Strike the Bell

transport by road, canal, rail and sea in the
nineteenth century through
songs, ballads and contemporary accounts

selected and edited by
ROY PALMER

CAMBRIDGE UNIVERSITY PRESS
Cambridge
London · New York · Melbourne

The Resources of Music Series

General Editors: *Wilfrid Mellers, John Paynter*

THE RESOURCES OF MUSIC *by Wilfrid Mellers*
SOUND AND SILENCE *by John Paynter and Peter Aston*
SOMETHING TO PLAY *by Geoffrey Brace*
MUSIC DRAMA IN SCHOOLS *edited by Malcolm John*
THE PAINFUL PLOUGH *by Roy Palmer*
THE VALIANT SAILOR *by Roy Palmer*
TROUBADOURS *by Brian Sargent*
MINSTRELS *by Brian Sargent*
POVERTY KNOCK *by Roy Palmer*
THE RIGS OF THE FAIR *by Roy Palmer and Jon Raven*
JAZZ *by Graham Collier*

POP MUSIC IN SCHOOL *edited by Graham Vulliamy and Ed Lee*
FOLK MUSIC IN SCHOOL *edited by Robert Leach and Roy Palmer*
VIBRATIONS *by David Sawyer*
MINSTRELS 2 *by Brian Sargent*

Recordings
SOUND AND SILENCE – record *John Paynter and Peter Aston*
TROUBADOURS AND MINSTRELS – record *Brian Sargent*
JAZZ: ILLUSTRATIONS – record *Graham Collier*
JAZZ: RHYTHM SECTION – tape *Graham Collier*
JAZZ: LECTURE CONCERT – record *Graham Collier*

Acknowledgements

Full source references to songs and prose passages are given on pp. 63-4. Sources of illustrations are listed on p. 64. The author and publisher would like to thank all those there listed for permission to reproduce material in this book.

While every effort has been made to contact copyright holders, the publishers apologise if any material has been included without permission.

For valuable assistance in the preparation of this book the author would like to thank the following: Sandra Kerr, for guitar chords; Katharine Thomson and Pat Palmer, for musical advice and assistance; Harry Boardman, Anthony Burton, Peter Freshwater, Keith Gregson, Roy Harris, Michael Honeybone, Rev. Hugh Hughes (Rector of Moelfre, Anglesey), Jon Raven, John Richards, the late Pat Shaw, Edward Thompson, Eric Twigg, Peter Wells, and Mike Yates. In addition, the librarians and staff of: Aberdeen University Library, Birmingham Reference Library, Birmingham University Library, Bodleian Library, British Library, Brown, Picton and Hornsby Libraries (Liverpool), Cambridge University Library, Cheshire Record Office, Leeds Central Library, Liverpool Record Office, Manchester Central Library, Mitchell Library (Glasgow), Museum of Inland Navigation (Ellesmere Port), National Maritime Museum, National Railway Museum, Newcastle upon Tyne University Library, Portsmouth Central Library, Sandeman Library (Perth), Westminster City Library.

Performing and recording rights are reserved and are administered by the Performing Rights Society, the Mechanical Copyright Protection Society and the affiliated bodies throughout the world. Applications should be made to these bodies for a relevant licence. Failure to so apply constitutes a breach of copyright.

The cover illustration shows an Easter Monday outing on a paddle steamer down the Thames in 1847.

The industrial token shown on the title page celebrates the opening of the Llanidloes and Newtown Railway in 1859.

CAMBRIDGE UNIVERSITY PRESS
Cambridge, New York, Melbourne, Madrid, Cape Town,
Singapore, São Paulo, Delhi, Tokyo, Mexico City

Cambridge University Press
The Edinburgh Building, Cambridge CB2 8RU, UK

Published in the United States of America by Cambridge University Press, New York

www.cambridge.org
Information on this title: www.cambridge.org/9780521219211

© Cambridge University Press 1978

This publication is in copyright. Subject to statutory exception
and to the provisions of relevant collective licensing agreements,
no reproduction of any part may take place without the written
permission of Cambridge University Press.

First published 1978
Re-issued 2011

A catalogue record for this publication is available from the British Library

Library of Congress Cataloguing in Publication data
Main entry under title:
Strike the bell.
(The Resources of music series)
SUMMARY: Songs and book and journal extracts depict travelling
by various modes in the nineteenth century.
1. Transportation – Songs and music. 2. Songs, English.
3. Ballads, English.
[1. Transportation – Songs and music. 2. Songs, English.
3. Ballads, English.]
[1. Transportation – Songs and music. 2. Songs, English.
3. Ballads, English. 4. Transportation.]
I. Palmer, Roy, 1932- II. Series.
M1977.T8S8   7846/8/3805   78-1282

ISBN 978-0-521-21921-1 Paperback

Cambridge University Press has no responsibility for the persistence or
accuracy of URLs for external or third-party internet websites referred to in
this publication, and does not guarantee that any content on such websites is,
or will remain, accurate or appropriate.

Contents

	Introduction	4
1	**The king's highway**	5
	Songs	
	1 The road makers	7
	2 The Buchan turnpike	8
	3 The Tantivy trot	11
	4 The jolly post-chaise boys	14
	5 The warbling waggoner	16
2	**The watery road**	18
	Songs	
	6 Grantham Navigation	20
	7 Paddy upon the canal	22
	8 The cruise of the 'Calabar'	26
3	**The iron road**	30
	Songs	
	9 Newcastle and Carlisle railway	32
	10 The Great Western railroad	36
	11 Railroad travelling	38
	12 Navvy on the line	42
	13 The iron horse	44
	14 The Greenock railway	46
4	**The ocean highway**	49
	Songs	
	15 The adventures of a steam packet	50
	16 The launch of the 'Great Britain'	52
	17 The wreck of the 'Royal Charter'	54
	18 The unseaworthy ship	58
	19 Strike the bell	60
	Suggestions for further activities	62
	Sources	63

Introduction

'Next after a fox-hunt,' wrote William Cobbett in 1816, 'the finest sight in the world is a stage-coach ready to start. A great sheep or cattle fair is a beautiful sight; but in the stage-coach you see more of what man is capable of performing.' Cobbett's fascination was partly aesthetic, but he was well aware of technical, social and economic considerations. The revolution in transport – on the roads, canals, railways and sea – not only played a major part in what we now call the Industrial Revolution, but was also a great human achievement in itself. The transport revolution was brought about by a cadre of skilled engineers and an army corps of workers. The engineers, often masters of several fields, constituted a previously unparalleled élite. Their story has been told in such books as L. T. C. Rolt's *Victorian Engineering*, and their achievements can still be seen in many parts of Britain.

The contribution made by ordinary working people has perhaps been less frequently recognised, though such books as Terry Coleman's *Railway Navvies* have begun to repair the omission. On the roads there were turnpike gate-men, coach drivers, guards, ostlers, innkeepers, waiters, cooks, clerks, carriage-builders, horse-breeders and harness-makers. The canals with their horse-drawn boats needed many similar people, with boatmen in charge instead of drivers. The railway needed a host of men, often highly skilled, including engine-drivers, signalmen, repairers of locomotives and rolling stock. Underpinning the vast pyramid were the labourers, soon to be called navvies (from 'inland navigators'). These were the men who built the roads, the canals and the railways, with picks, shovels, wheelbarrows, and, apart from some assistance from explosives and from horse power, with their own strength and courage. Their equivalent at sea were the men before the mast, who took the view that to go to sea for pleasure was equivalent to going to hell for pastime.

This book attempts to show something of the attitudes of those who made and ran British transport systems, and of those who travelled, through extracts from contemporary accounts, juxtaposed with songs and ballads. To a modern traveller at least, it is extraordinary to realise that in the past songs were not only a commentary on, but part of the very texture of, everyday life. Stage-coach passengers, at least those in the cheaper, outside seats, sang to while away the hours of travel. Many guards played tunes on their coach horns. A journalist writing on the canals in 1858 noted that 'the boatmen at the tillers nearly all sing'. He observed the popularity of 'the plaintive ballad', which he attributed to 'the fact that it generally contains a story, and is written in a measure that fits easily into a slow, drawling, breath-taking tune which all the lower orders know'. (This tune – which I am often accused of singing – is, in reality, a whole variety of folk tunes.)

Sailing-ship sailors sang a great deal. Shanties were the songs whose rhythms were precisely suited to the various tasks involved in working a ship. They were not merely utilitarian, but often had 'the nobility of great poetry' as John Masefield once said. Seamen, on steamships as well as sailing ships, also had forebitters, songs for their leisure and pleasure, which often included tales of shipwreck and storm. Navvies apparently did not sing very much while at work, but made up for it at play. One navvy and his wife fell short of money while tramping the country, so the wife sang in the streets of Warwick, and made four shillings and ninepence in an hour, as much as a couple of days' pay.

Railwaymen, on the other hand, seem to have sung very little. They were renowned for their addiction to their work: 'railways went through the back of your spine like Blackpool went through rock', said an engine-driver, as recently as 1957. Yet, perhaps because the industry was so new, perhaps because so many men – drivers, guards, signalmen, for example – worked alone or in ones and twos, they did not sing about their work, or, with a few rare exceptions, what they sang has not survived. Railways are nevertheless well represented by songs from travellers and navvies.

The passengers and workers did not confine themselves to songs about particular modes of transport. Much of what they sang was the general repertoire of the day, a mixture of subjects and of styles, from folk song, via street ballad and local anthem to sentimental ditty. This is not a general book, however, but one about transport, so all the songs chosen are about this topic. On the whole, singers were less interested in the technology of transport than in its social and human aspects and implications. Songs helped to express the impact of change, to assimilate it, humanise it, and thus make sense of it. In so doing they convey, with freshness and immediacy, the reactions of those who were involved with this transport revolution.

These songs, like the material legacies of the industrial revolution, are part of our heritage. Perhaps they can help us to understand the past, and thus shed light on the present.

1
The king's highway

The road maker

In the year 1751, Metcalf commenced a new employ: He set up a stage waggon between York and Knaresborough, being the first on that road, and conducted it constantly himself, twice a week in the summer season, and once in winter; and this business, together with the occasional conveyance of army baggage, employed his attention until the period of his first contracting for the making of roads, which suiting him better, he disposed of his draught, and interest in the road, to one Guiseley.

An act of Parliament having been obtained to make a road from Harrogate to Boroughbridge, a person of the name of Ostler, of Farnham, two miles from Knaresborough, a man of great ability, and who had great confidence confided in him, was appointed surveyor; Metcalf falling into company with him, agreed to make about three miles of it, viz. between Minskip and Fearnsby. The materials were to be procured from one gravel-pit for the whole length: he therefore provided deal boards and erected a temporary house at the pit, took a dozen horses to the place, fixed racks and mangers; and hired a house for his men at Minskip, which was distant about three-quarters of a mile. He often walked from Knaresborough in the morning, with four or five stone of meat on his shoulders, and joined his men by six o'clock: and by the means he used, he completed the work much sooner than was expected, to the entire satisfaction of the surveyor and trustees.

Soon after, there was a mile and a half of turnpike-road to be made between Knaresborough-Bridge and Harrogate, which Metcalf also agreed for. Going one day over a place covered with grass, he told his men that he thought it different from the ground adjoining, and would have them try for stone or gravel, which they immediately did, and found an old causeway, supposed to have been made in the time of the Romans, which afforded many materials proper for the purpose of making the road. Between the Forest-Lane head and Knaresborough-Bridge, there was a bog, in a low piece of ground, over which to have passed was the nearest way; and the surveyor thought it impossible to make a road over it: but Metcalf assured him that he could easily accomplish it. The other then told him, that if so, he should be paid for the same length as if he had gone round. Jack set about it, cast the road up, and covered it with whin and ling; made it as good or better, than any part he had undertaken. He received about four hundred pounds for the road and a small bridge which he had built over a brook called Stanbeck.

A road was then advertised to be let from Wakefield to

Austerland, intended to lead through Horbury, Almondbury, Huddersfield, Marsden and Saddleworth, which was the Manchester road. A meeting was held at Huddersfield, for the purpose. At that time none of the road was marked out, except between Marsden and Standish-Foot, leading over a common called Pule and Standish; the surveyor took it over deep marshes; but Metcalf not expecting it to have been carried that way, thought it a great hardship, and complained to the gentleman; but knowing that it would be to little purpose to hold a contest with them, he said, 'Gentlemen, I propose to make the road over the marshes, after my own plan; and if it does not answer, I will be at the expence of making it over again, after your's': which was consented to. And as he had engaged to make nine miles of the road in ten months, he began in six different parts, with nearly four hundred men employed. One of the places was Pule and Standish common, being a deep bog and thought impracticable to make a road over, which he cast fourteen yards wide, and raised in a circular form. Water in several places ran across the road, which he carried off by drains; but found the greatest difficulty in conveying stones to the places for the purpose, on account of the softness of the ground.*

*The road from Wakefield to Austerlands (which is part of Oldham, now called Scout Head, though a road sign marked 'Austerlands' still exists) was constructed in 1759. The nine-mile stretch mentioned is probably that between Longroyd Bridge and Marsden. Pule Hill is slightly beyond Marsden; Standish is probably a misunderstanding for Stanedge (locally pronounced 'Stanidge'). The route followed was not in the valley bottom, but well up the hillside, to avoid drainage difficulties. It coincided with an earlier bridle path. (I am indebted to Mr Eric Twigg and his colleagues at Huddersfield Polytechnic for this information.)

Road making. Both the pictures in this section are from Pyne's Microcosm, *published in 1808*

Numbers of clothiers usually going that way to Huddersfield market were by no means sparing in their censure, and held much diversity of opinion, relative to its completion. But Metcalf got the piece levelled to the end, having sixty men employed, but wanted to keep the manner of their proceeding as secret as possible, but will now make it known, as it may be useful to any person who chuses to pursue the plan: he ordered his men to pull and bind heather, or ling, in round bundles, that they could span with their hands, and directed them to lay it on the intended road, by placing the bundles in rows, and laying another upon each, pressing them well down; as the carts were obliged to come on and go off at one end, he always kept it covered in this manner, with ling for the carriages to turn upon. He then brought broad-wheeled carts, and began to lead stone and gravel for covering. When the first load was brought and laid on, and the horses had gone off in safety, the company huzza'd from surprise. They completed the whole of this length, which was about half a mile; and it was so particularly fine, that any person might have gone over it in winter, unshod, without being wet. This piece of road needed no repairs for twelve years afterwards, but the other parts of the road wanted repairing immediately after.

In 1789 he was informed that there was a great quantity of road to let in Lancashire: he accordingly went, and took a part between Bury and Estlington, and another part from Estlington to Ackrington; also a branch from that to Blackburn. There were such hollows to fill, and hills to be taken down, to form the level, as was never done before: in several of the hollows the walls were ten yards high, before the battlements were put on the top. He had two summers allowed to finish this work in; but the trade in Lancashire being brisk, made wages very high, and the navigation at that time cutting through country so employed the men, that it was a very difficult matter to procure a sufficiency of hands. The first summer the rains were so perpetual, that he lost about two hundred pounds; but in the next he completed the whole work, and received by the hands of Mr Carr, of Blackburn, three thousand five hundred pounds; and, after all, was forty pounds loser by it. (*The Life of John Metcalf*, 2nd edn. 1801.)

Metcalf (1717-1810) was perhaps better known as Blind Jack of Knaresborough. Despite his blindness, caused by smallpox when he was six, he was an intrepid walker, swimmer and horse-rider. He was a proficient musician, playing the fiddle and hautboy (oboe), and was employed for a time as Harrogate town fiddler, to play for country dancing. He was interested in all kinds of sport, and frequently rode to hounds. He was a great betting man, and a joker. He eloped with the lady whom he married. Apart from music and wagers, Metcalf made a living from all sorts of business ventures. In the latter part of his life, apparently with little preparation, he entered the road-making business and successfully contructed some 150 miles of road, as well as many bridges, drains, culverts and turnpike houses.

Song 1 *The road makers*

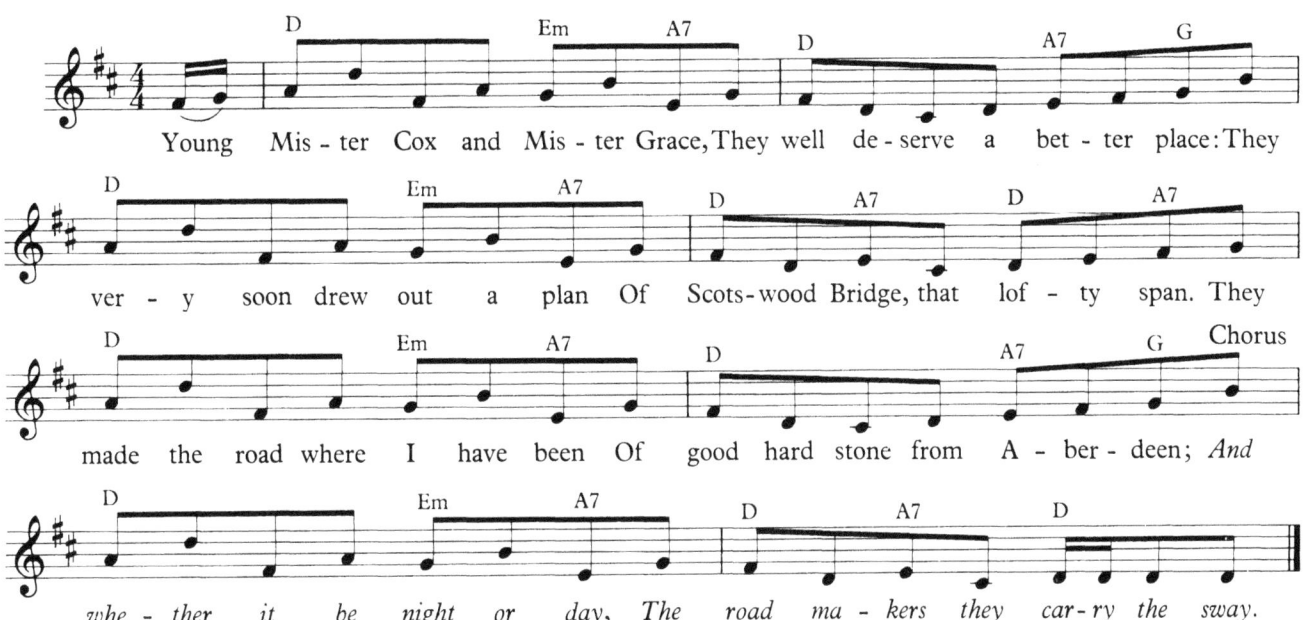

Young Mister Cox and Mister Grace, They well deserve a better place: They very soon drew out a plan Of Scotswood Bridge, that lofty span. They made the road where I have been Of good hard stone from Aberdeen; And whether it be night or day, The road makers they carry the sway.

2 From Newcastle to Elswick Dean
　The road is like a bowling green;
　From Elswick Dean to Paradise
　The road is formed out so nice;
　From Paradise up to Scotswood
　The plan it is extremely good.

3 The navvy men with hacks and spades,
　They are a few of roving blades;
　They fill the barrows on the plank
　And wheel them up to raise a bank.
　When they have got the ready chink
　They will not fail to have a drink.

4 The carters, too, with whip in hand,
　They have the horses at command;
　They feed them up with corn and hay
　And load them well throughout the day.
　They mount a horse and ride away
　To get some drink before the pay.

5 The stone-breakers, when you pass by,
　They hit the stones and make them fly;
　When they are standing on their feet
　They break them all, both small and great.
　No man alive can them control;
　They love to drink a flowing bowl.

6 Not long ago the rising flood
　Did try the road how firm it stood;
　The grand footpath along the side
　Is formed out near six foot wide:
　A pleasant walk up through the vale,
　Where boats and keels and wherries sail.

Mr Cox and Mr Grace: Mr Grace was a surveyor and Mr Cox may have been his assistant. Chink: money. Keels: boats which carried coal down the Tyne for transhipment to sea-going vessels. Wherries: another type of boat.

　The road celebrated here was the turnpike from Newcastle upon Tyne via such places as Elswick Dean, Paradise and Scotswood Bridge to Blaydon; it was surveyed in 1828. There was previously a foot road, and travellers crossed the Tyne at Scotswood by ferry. The new Scotswood road and bridge later became famous through another song, George Ridley's *Blaydon Races* (1864). In 1828 the road would have cost about £600 a mile to construct, which contrasts with the figure of £1½ million a mile for a motorway 150 years later.

Song 2 The Buchan turnpike

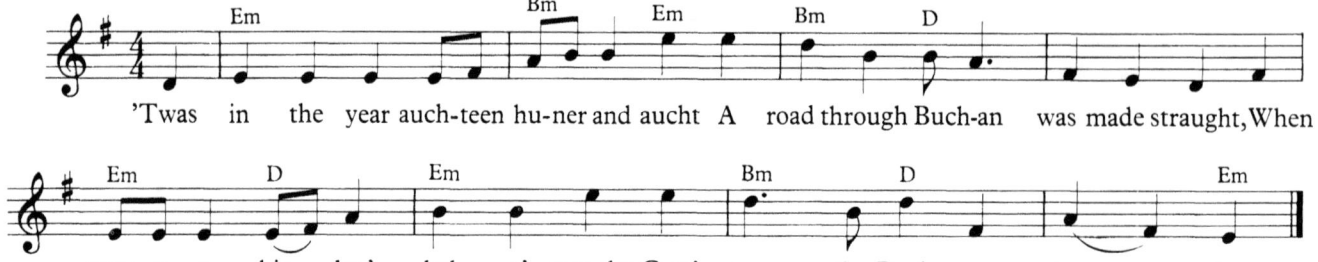

'Twas in the year auchteen hu-ner and aucht A road through Buch-an was made straught, When mon-y a hie-lan' lad o' maught Cam' owre the Buch-an bor-der.

2 'Twixt Peterhead and Banff's ould toon
It twines the knowes and hollows roon;
Ye scarce can tell its ups frae doon,
It's levelled in sic order.

3 The hielan' and the lowlan' chiels
Cut doon the knowes wi' spads and sheels,
And bored the stanes wi' jumpin' dreels
To get the road in order.

4 There was some in tartan, some in blue,
Wi' weskits o' a warlike hue,
And werena they a strappin' crew
To put the road in order?

5 And mony a hup and mony a ban
Got cartin' horse and lazy man,
For fou and teem and aye they ran
To push't a bittie forder.

6 Chiel Chalmers he frae Strichen cam',
Wi' ae black horse as bold's a ram;
Nae ane could match him in the tram:
He made a braw recorder.

7 The Meerisons, the Wichts and Giels,
Were swack and willin' workin' chiels,
Sae weel's they banged the barrow steels
To gar the road gae forder.

8 The road's as smooth's a harrowed rig,
Wi' stankies on ilk side fu' trig;
And ilk bit burn has noo a brig
Where ance we had to ford 'er.

9 This turnpike it will be a boon
To a' the quintra roon and roon,
And lat folk gae and come frae toon
Wi' easedom and wi' order.

10 On fit ye're owre it free to stray,
But if a beast ye chance to hae
At ilka sax miles ye maun pay
For gaun a bittie forder.

11 The writer's name gin ye should spier,
I'm Jamie Shirran frae New Deer,
A name well kent baith far and near,
I dwell near the road's border.

To a non-Scot this song might appear rather impenetrable, but it repays a little effort. Auchteen huner and aucht: eighteen hundred and eight. Straught: straight. Mony: many. Heilan': highland. Maught: might. Knowes: hillocks. Sic: such. Chiels: men (the reference is to the road labourers, or navvies). Spads and sheels: spades and picks. Stanes: stones. Dreels: drills. Hup and ... ban: grunt and groan. Fou and teem and aye they ran: to fill and empty still they ran. A bittie forder: a bit further. Tram: a cart. Chalmers ... made a braw recorder: the reference may be to George Chalmers, the Buchan antiquary who was alive at that time. Perhaps Chalmers wrote something about the turnpike. Swack: nimble. To gar the road gae forder: to make the road go further. Rig: field. Stankies on ilk side fu' trig: ditches on each side so trim. Ilk bit burn: each little brook. Quintra: country. Ilka sax miles ye maun pay: every six miles you must pay. Spier: ask. I'm Jamie Shirran: John Shirran (a local bard who lived at New Deer, Aberdeenshire, and died in the 1840s at an advanced age). Kent: known.

This song was sung in Aberdeenshire for at least a century. Gavin Greig made this comment: 'The making of a turnpike road, however important an event in its own way, hardly looks a subject for verse; and nowadays one could scarcely imagine a bard condescending on such a prosaic theme. It must be remembered, however, that long ago the ballad was the only vehicle available for historical record; and the song before us simply illustrates the revival of this practice of keeping up the memory of notable events by making a rhyme about them and getting it sung. And look how the plan has succeeded in the present case. For any number of people throughout Buchan know about the making of the Peterhead and Banff turnpike from this song and from no other source of information' (*Folk-Song of the North-East*, 1909 and 1914).

The word 'turnpike' is still used with the meaning of 'main road' in America and, by some old people, in this country. Originally a turnpike was a sort of turnstile with pikes attached which revolved on top of a post and acted as a barrier. Later the name was transferred to the gates on certain roads, then to the roads themselves. Resentment at paying tolls was by no means confined to Scotland. Gates were destroyed in protest on a number of occasions, the most famous being in Wales during the Rebecca Riots of 1839 and 1842-3. Travellers (other than those on foot) had to stop at the gates to pay tolls, which were used for the upkeep of the roads. Any profit would go to the turnpike trust responsible for the particular stretch of road. The first Act of Parliament authorising the turnpiking of roads was in 1663. In the next century a great many turnpike trusts were set up by private act. A General Turnpike Act was passed in 1773 to simplify the process. It was not until 1888 that the responsibility for main roads passed to county councils.

The turnpikes eventually led to the great age of coaching. Stage coaches had existed from the mid-seventeenth century, but they remained in very small numbers until about a hundred years later. By the first quarter of the nineteenth century Britain had the finest public transport system in the world, thanks to the stage coach and the turnpike road. In 1824, for example, some 1500 coaches were leaving London daily, including 40 to Brighton, over 40 to Birmingham, nearly 20 to Chester, almost 60 to Liverpool, 18 to York, and 12 each to Hull and Preston.

Tyburn turnpike in 1813

Stage-coach adventures

INSIDE. Crammed full of passengers – three fat, fusty, old men – a young mother and sick child – a cross old maid – a poll parrot – a bag of red herrings – double-barrelled gun (which you are afraid is loaded) – and a snarling lap-dog, in addition to yourself – awaking out of a sound nap, with the cramp in one leg, and the other in a lady's band-box – pay the damage (four or five shillings) for 'gallantry's sake' – getting out in the dark, at the half-way house, in the hurry stepping into the return coach, and finding yourself the next morning at the spot you had started from the evening before – not a breath of air – asthmatic old man, and a child with the measles – windows closed in consequence – unpleasant smell – shoes filled with warm water – look up and: find it's the child – obliged to bear it – no appeal – shut your eyes, and scold the dog – pretend sleep, and pinch the child – mistake – pinch the dog, and get bit – execrate the child in return – black looks – 'no gentleman' – pay the coachman, and drop a piece of gold in the straw – not to be found – fell through a crevice – coachman says, 'he'll find it' – can't – get out yourself – gone – picked up by the ostler. – No time for 'blowing up' – coach off for next stage – lose your money – get in – lose your seat – stuck in the middle – get laughed at – lose your temper – turn sulky, and turned over in a horse-pond.

INSIDE AND OUTSIDE. Drunken coachman – horse sprawling – wheel off – pole breaking, down hill – axle-tree splitting – coach over-turning – winter, and buried in the snow – one eye poked out with an umbrella, the other cut open by the broken window – reins breaking – impudent guard – hurried at meals – imposition of inn-keepers – five minutes and a half to swallow three and sixpennyworth of vile meat – waiter a rogue – 'Like master, like man' – half a bellyful, and frozen to death – internal grumblings and outward complaints – no redress – walk forward while the horses are changing – take the wrong turning – lose yourself and lose the coach – goodbye to portmanteau – curse your ill-luck – wander about in the dark road and find the inn at last – get upon the next coach going the same road – stop at the next inn – brandy and water, hot, to keep you in spirits – warm fire – pleasant company – heard the guard cry 'All right?' – run out, just in time to sing out 'I'm left', as the coach turns the corner – after it 'full tear' – come up with it, at the end of a mile – get up, 'all in a blowze' – catch cold – sore throat – inflammation – doctor – warm bath – fever – DIE. (Article signed 'Gaspard' in William Hone, *Every-Day and Table Book*, vol. III, 1838).

There were accidents in plenty with stage coaches, as they quickened in speed. Ten or eleven miles per hour became common on macadamised turnpikes and on May Day 1830, by travelling from London to Birmingham, a distance of 109 miles, in seven and a half hours, a coach attained the record average speed over a long haul of $14\frac{1}{2}$ m.p.h. This was the Independent Tally-ho mentioned by George Eliot, who was by no means the only writer to think highly of coaching days. Dickens frequently describes journeys by coach, particularly in *The Pickwick Papers* (first published 1836-7), and there is a famous chapter on the subject in Thomas Hughes' *Tom Brown's Schooldays* (1856).

Currency

Sums of money mentioned in the text are in terms of pounds, shillings and pence. Here is a brief guide to their decimal equivalents:

The old sixpence (6d.) = $2\frac{1}{2}$p
The old shilling (1s.) = 5p
Ten shillings (10s.) = 50p
One pound (20s.) = £1.00

12 old pence (12d.) = 1 shilling (1s.)
20 shillings (20s.) = 1 pound (£1.0.0)
21 shillings = 1 guinea
2 shillings and sixpence = half-a-crown

Coaches and coach fares in 1789

Coaches to London, Bath, and Chester, left Dudley and Palmer's Original Hotel, Temple Row [Birmingham], on Mondays, Wednesdays, and Fridays, the fares being 19s. inside and 9s. 6d. outside to Chester, 24s. and 13s. to London, and 27s. and 14s. to Bath. From the Dog Inn, Spiceal Street, coaches left every day for Derby, Nottingham, and Sheffield, arriving there in time to meet the coaches going north, the fares to Sheffield being 21s. and 12s. From the George Inn, coaches for London and for Shrewsbury went every Monday, Wednesday, and Friday; to Leicester on Tuesday and Thursday, meeting vehicles for Stamford, Lincoln, Peterborough, Boston, &c.; to Warwick on Wednesday and Saturday; the fares to Shrewsbury were 12s. and 6s., Leicester 12s. and 7s., Hinckley 9s. and 5s., Coventry 6s. and 3s., Warwick 5s. 6d. and 3s. From the Castle Inn the mail coach for Oxford and London started every evening, doing the distance in sixteen hours for 30s.; Bristol and Bath every evening: Shrewsbury and Holyhead on Tuesday, Thursday and Saturday mornings: Derby, Nottingham, and Sheffield every morning; Buxton, Ashburn, and Manchester on Monday, Wednesday, and Friday mornings; Coventry, Worcester, and Wolverhampton each having its daily coach. The London coach from the Castle yard put up at the George and Blue Boar, Holborn, from whence the Dover coaches and 'diligences' started morning and evening. The travellers for Paris could also go from the White Bear, Piccadilly, at five o'clock in the morning on Monday, Thursday, and Saturday at a cost of five guineas each for carriage, sea passage, diet and lodging, though should they be detained at Dover by contrary winds they had to pay their own expenses from the next day of their arrival to the time of their shipping. (*Swinney's Chronicle*.)

Song 3 *The Tantivy trot*

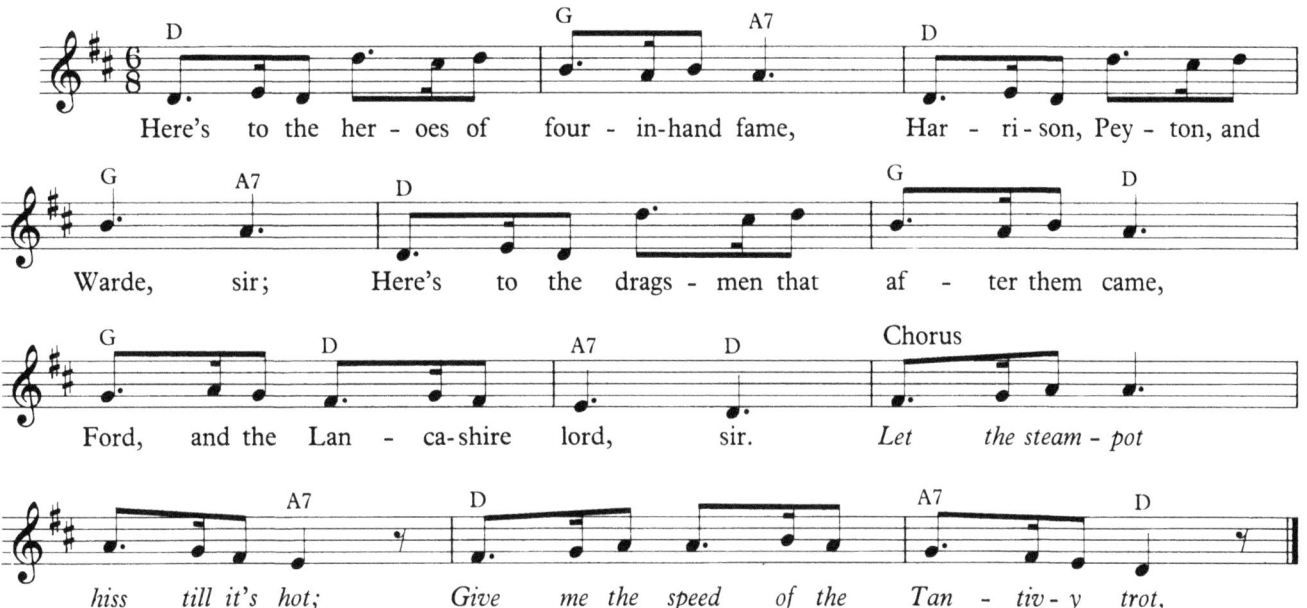

2. Here's to the team, sir, all harnessed to start,
   Brilliant in Brummagem leather;
   Here's to the waggoner skilled in the art
   Of coupling the cattle together.

3. Here's to the arm that holds them when gone,
   Still to a gallop inclined, sir;
   Heads to the front with no bearing reins on,
   Tails with no cruppers behind, sir.

4. Here's to the shape that is shown the near side,
   Here's to the blood on the off, sir;
   Limbs without check to the freedom of stride,
   Wind without whistle or cough, sir.

5. Here's to the dear little damsels within,
   Here's to the swells on the top, sir;
   Here's to the music of three feet of tin,
   Here's to the tapering top, sir.

6. Here's to the dragsmen I've dragged into song,
   Salisbury, Mountain and Co., sir;
   Here's to the Cracknell that cracks 'em along,
   Five twenty times at a go, sir.

7. Here's to MacAdams, the Mac of all Macs,
   Here's to the road we ne'er tire on;
   Let me but roll o'er the granite he cracks,
   Ride ye who like it on iron.

Four-in-hand: stage coaches were pulled by four horses, and the drivers therefore had four sets of reins to manage. Harrison, Peyton and Warde: drivers; the last two are probably Sir Henry Peyton, a well-known amateur, and the veteran coachman, Charles Ward (1810-99). Dragsmen: another term for coach drivers. Ford, and the Lancashire lord: not traced; the latter might be one of the sporting men to bear the name of Lord Derby. Coupling the cattle: harnessing the team. Bearing rein: rein fixed from bit to saddle. Crupper: strap under horse's tail. See page 12 for a picture of a coach team in harness. Shape: poor horse. Blood: fine horse. Three feet of tin: coach horn. Salisbury: coachman. Mountain and Co.: coach firm. Cracknell: coachman (see below). MacAdams: John Loudon McAdam (1756-1836), Scotsman who invented the macadam road surface to which he gave his name. On iron: on the railway.

The Tantivy was the name of a coach service between London and Birmingham, which started in 1832. Coaches left the Blossoms Inn at Cheapside, London, at seven in the morning and arrived at Birmingham twelve hours later. They travelled via Maidenhead, Henley, Oxford, Woodstock, Shipston-on-Stour and Stratford-on-Avon. With an hour off for changing horses and for taking refreshments, the distance of 125 miles was covered at an average speed of just over 11 m.p.h. Cracknell, the most famous of the Tantivy coachmen, usually drove from London to Oxford, though on one occasion he drove the whole way to Birmingham. However, Harry Salisbury usually drove from Oxford to Birmingham. Of course, many other drivers were needed to maintain the service.

The song, to the tune of 'Here's to the maiden of bashful fifteen', was written in 1834 by R. E. Egerton Warburton (1803-91) of Arley, Cheshire. It reflects the great vogue for coach driving among fashionable young men at the time, when 'the education of no gay young blood was complete until he had acquired the art of four-in-hand driving. A "real gentleman" was one who flung away his money in tips, and many "young oxonians" or "young cantabs" . . . were frequent aspirants for the ribbons. Not unnaturally professional coachmen on the Oxford and Cambridge roads made plenty of hard cash out of this enthusiasm, but the passengers saw it very differently, galloping at the incredible speed of 20 m.p.h., the coach rocking violently, while the outsides held on like frightened men, and the insides prayed for a safe arrival. Coach proprietors dreaded the amateurs and instantly dismissed any coachman in their employ who allowed one to drive' (R. C. and J. M. Anderson, *Quicksilver*, 1973, p. 51).

The Cambridge Telegraph stage coach loaded with undergraduates outside a London tavern. The picture was published in the 1830s

A heavily loaded stage waggon. Waggons like these were common in the eighteenth and nineteenth centuries before the coming of the railways

The stage waggon

They arranged to proceed upon their journey next evening, as a stage waggon, which travelled for some distance on the same road as they must take, would stop at the inn to change horses, and the driver for a small gratuity would give Nell a place inside. A bargain was soon struck when the waggon came; and in due time it rolled away; with the child comfortably bestowed among the softer packages, her grandfather and the schoolmaster walking on beside the driver, and the landlady and all the good folks of the inn screaming out their good wishes and farewells.

What a soothing, luxurious, drowsy way of travelling, to lie inside that slowly-moving mountain, listening to the tinkling of the horses' bells, the occasional smacking of the carter's whip, the smooth rolling of the great broad wheels, the rattle of the harness, the cheery good-nights of passing travellers jogging past on little short-stepped horses – all made pleasantly indistinct by the thick awning, which seemed made for lazy listening under, till one fell asleep! The very going to sleep, still with an indistinct idea, as the head jogged to and fro upon the pillow, of moving forward with no trouble or fatigue, and hearing all these sounds like dreamy music, lulling to the senses – and the slow waking up, and finding one's self staring out through the breezy curtain half-opened in the front, far up into the cold bright sky with its countless stars, and downward at the driver's lantern dancing on like its namesake, Jack of the swamps and marshes, and sideways at the dark grim trees, and forward at the long bare road rising up, up, up, until it stopped abruptly at a sharp high ridge as if there were no more road, and all beyond was sky – and the stopping at an inn to bait, and being helped out, and going into a room with fire and candles, and winking very much, and being agreeably reminded that the night was cold, and anxious for very comfort's sake to think it colder than it was! – What a delicious journey was that journey in the waggon.

Then the going on again – so fresh at first, and shortly afterwards so sleepy. The waking from a sound nap as the mail came dashing past like a highway comet, with gleaming lamps and rattling hoofs, and visions of a guard behind, standing up to keep his feet warm, and of a gentleman in a fur cap opening his eyes and looking wild and stupefied – the stopping at the turnpike where the man was gone to bed, and knocking at the door until he answered with a smothered shout from under the bed-clothes in the little room above, where the faint light was burning, and presently came down, night-capped and shivering, to throw the gate wide open, and wish all waggons off the road, except by day. The cold sharp interval between night and morning – the distant streak of light widening and spreading, and turning from grey to white, and from white to yellow, and from yellow to burning red – the presence of day, with all its cheerfulness and life – men and horses at the plough – birds in the trees and hedges, and boys in solitary fields, frightening them away with rattles. The coming to a town – people busy in the markets; light carts and chaises round the tavern yard; tradesmen standing at their doors; men running horses up and down the street for sale; pigs plunging and grunting in the dirty distance, getting off with long strings at their legs, running into clean chemists' shops and being dislodged with brooms by 'prentices; the night coach changing horses – the passengers cheerless, cold, ugly, and discontented, with three months' growth of hair in one night – the coachman fresh as from a band-box, and exquisitely beautiful by contrast – so much bustle, so many things in motion, such a variety of incidents – when was there a journey with so many delights as that journey in the waggon!
(Charles Dickens, *The Old Curiosity Shop*, 1841, ch. 46.)

Song 4 *The jolly post-chaise boys*

2. Now there is six good horses that's kept at this place,
   And two jolly lads for to drive from stage to stage.
   For ninepence a mile day and night you may fly
   Over hills and over dales till fair Nottingham you spy.

3. Our horses they are fed off the best corn and hay,
   With good litters for to lay upon by night and by day;
   They're kept so very clean from the head to the feet,
   And such accommodation you seldom do meet.

4. Oh it's when I do return with an empty chaise,
   If I meet with a pretty girl upon her I will gaze;
   Saying, 'My dear, will you get up beside me for to bide?
   For here you see a turn-back chaise if you choose for to ride.'

5. With a little persuasion then up she doth get;
   He soon follows after and down by her doth sit,
   Saying, 'My dear, your countenance I should like to enjoy,
   For to have ride for ride you cannot me deny.'

6. With a little persuasion he on her doth prevail,
   And what followed after's not my province to tell tales.
   'The joys of my heart, we have both played our part';
   She said, 'Such jolly lads as you have fairly won my heart.'

7. When they come to an inn down by her he doth sit;
   Good liquor she gives him her health for to drink,
   Saying, 'My dear, I pray tell me, your name I'd like to know.'
   'Oh, it's Robin in the Rushes, and you may call me so.'

8 So now to conclude and finish my new song,
   O'er hills and o'er dales till we spy fair Nottingham;
   When we come to an inn it's there that we shall take our fill,
   Drink a health to Robin Hood, Little John, and likewise Will.

Post-chaise boys: the post-chaise was a light carriage drawn by up to four horses, and available for private hire. It would travel only one stage before returning to base (see verse 4), after leaving the passengers to transfer to another vehicle. The driver, who would ride on one of the horses, was called a post-boy, though he was neither a boy nor anything to do with letters: 'post' here refers to the practice of travelling in relays.

The song was printed sometime between 1818 and 1835. Here are some remarks published a little earlier, in 1808:

'Combined with our excellent roads, our post-chaise is certainly a great luxury in travelling. [It] is equally easy, expeditious, and safe: we mean safe as to over-turning or breaking down; for with respect to those unlicensed assessors on the king's highway, footpads and highwaymen, it is rather dangerous, particularly in the neighbourhood of London. It attracts them from the idea that it is generally the more wealthy who travel in it, and at the most there can seldom be above three in it, while the chance is in favour of their being fewer, and that there may be a female, or perhaps two.

'To a single traveller post-chaising it is very expensive, but to three it costs little more than travelling by stage. We must notice here the increased expense arising from the money given to the post-boy. This, at an average, is not less now than three-pence a mile, or the one-fifth of what is paid to his master for the use of the horses and the chaise. The plea for committing this extravagance is that it makes the boy drive faster and with more care. This effect may very well be doubted. Servants never pay so much attention when the master begins to bribe. The real effect is to render them mercenary and indolent.

'A post-chaise and pair will go 7 or 8 miles an hour with ease, as we phrase it: how the poor animals themselves would phrase it, could they give us their opinion, is another matter. A post-chaise and four, which is travelling in its best style, will go 10 miles at an average, as they keep running on without any diminution of their pace even up rising grounds, except these be uncommonly steep.

'The life of a post-horse is a most pitiable one. Often foundered, spavined, broken-winded, galled, in the scorching heat of summer as in the piercing cold of winter, but the latter indeed they do not feel, wet or dry, covered with dust or dirt, at all times of night or day, they must go from 6 to 10 miles an hour. The mail-coach horse draws in a heavy vehicle, and is forced to go at a severe rate; but the number of miles which it plies is fixed and regular, and generally does not exceed 12 at a spell. When this is performed, it is at ease till the fixed hour for plying returns. But there is no settled distance or rest for the post-horse. The moment it comes in from one stage, frequently it has to set off again on another. During elections and races its life becomes pure misery. Even in ordinary times, the distance which the poor animal goes day after day is cruel: 30 miles one day, 50 the next, and perhaps 40 the third. No traveller of sensibility will ever wish the post-boy to ride [on one of the horses]. This is additional cruelty to one of the poor horses: and the other is affected by it, as a horse cannot both carry a rider and exert the same degree of force in drawing too, as when without a rider. It may be stylish, but it is not humane.' (Commentary by G. Gray on drawings by W. H. Pyne published in his *Microcosm*, 1808.)

A halfpenny token, about 1792, celebrating the introduction of mail coaches which ran in stages along main routes and revolutionised the postal service in Britain

Song 5 *The warbling waggoner*

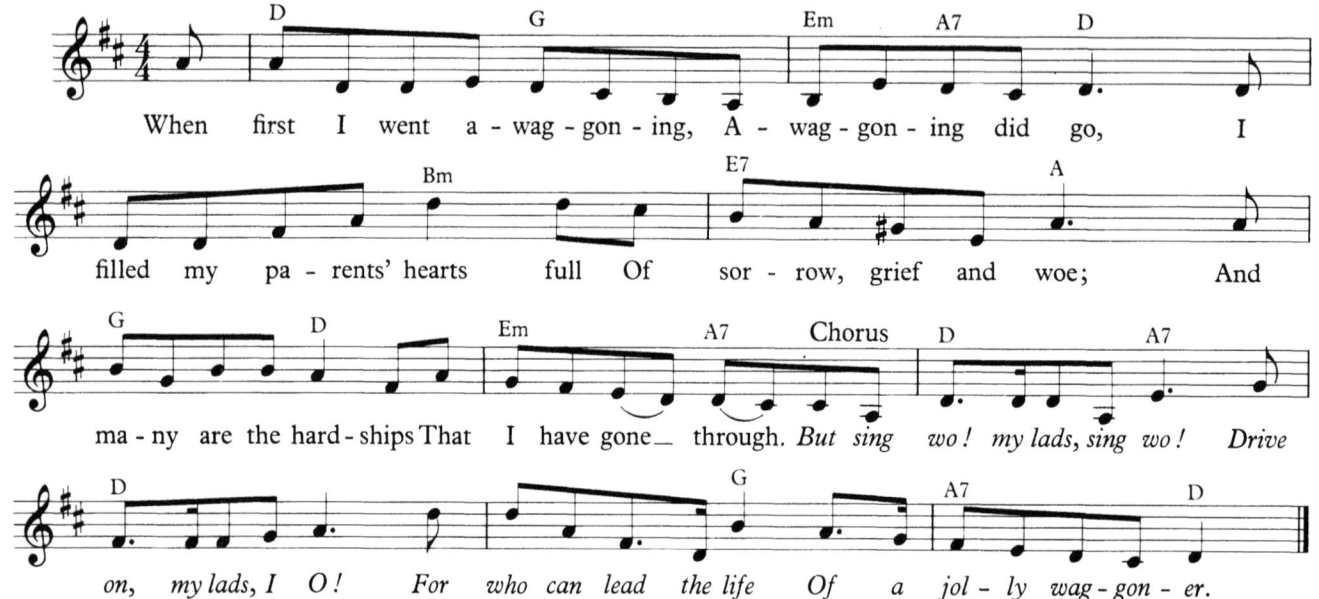

When first I went a-wag-gon-ing, A-wag-gon-ing did go, I filled my pa-rents' hearts full Of sor-row, grief and woe; And ma-ny are the hard-ships That I have gone through. *But sing wo! my lads, sing wo! Drive on, my lads, I O! For who can lead the life Of a jol-ly wag-gon-er.*

2 It is a dark and stormy night
   And I'm wet to the skin,
   But I'll bear it with contentment
   Till I get to the inn.
   Then I will get a-drinking
   With the landlord and his friends.
   And sing, *etc.*

3 Now summer it is coming,
   What pleasure we shall see;
   The small birds are singing
   In every green tree;
   The blackbirds and thrushes
   Are whistling in the grove.
   Then sing, *etc.*

4 Now Michaelmas is coming,
   What pleasures we shall find,
   We'll make the gold to fly, my boys,
   Like chaff before the wind;
   And every lad shall have his lass
   And set her on his knee.
   And sing, *etc.*

5 But now upon the country roads
   Few waggons there you'll see;
   The world's turned topsy-turvy
   And all things go by steam.
   The public now they all cry out,
   'Whatever shall we do?'
   So sing, *etc.*

6 The railway has taken the trade,
   It's made worse than before:
   It's made it better for one or two
   And ruined many a score;
   But I will not let my heart down,
   So come join me in my song,
   And sing, *etc.*

Michaelmas: 29 September; formerly the end of the farming year in some areas, after which workers could offer themselves for hire for another year with the same or a different employer, and would receive an advance of salary. The other reason for gold to be flying (verse 4) is that bonuses and overtime earned during harvest would be paid at the end of September.

Stage coaches, and still more, post-chaises, were too expensive for ordinary people to use. Therefore they either walked or used the market (or carriers') carts. Indeed, these conveyances, mainly intended for carrying goods, travelled barely faster than walking pace. The waggoners were popular figures who did pleasant things like decorating their horses and themselves with coloured ribbons on May Day. The 'Jolly Waggoner' was not uncommon as as inn-sign, and waggoners had something of a reputation as singers, perhaps to while away the long hours of their journeys.

This song, which is more usually entitled *The Jolly Waggoner*, probably started life in the late eighteenth century, when it had only four verses (the first four here). The advent of railways caused the last two to be added, probably in the late 1830s or early 1840s. While the railways undoubtedly killed off the stage coach and the stage waggon, both lingered a while in remote areas. There is a fine account of a journey which took place in 1864 from King's Lynn to London and back, in W. H. Barrett's *Tales from the Fens* (Routledge, 1963). The carrier's cart lasted still longer.

A ride in the carrier's cart

I was born on 7 February 1914. I can remember going to our market town, Salisbury, in the carrier's cart. My uncle, Lewis White, was proprietor and driver, and he made the journey twice a week, on Tuesdays and Saturdays. Reaching the town, six miles away, needed two-and-a-half hours, and when, after the first two miles, we could see at last the telegraph wires on their tall poles by the side of the main Salisbury-to-London road we were inclined to cheer. They were our first glimpse of the outside world.

We sat on hard seats, facing each other, under the waterproof tilt of the cart, which was really a smallish waggon. As a rule, aged or pregnant women and small children were the only passengers. Able-bodied men and women found it quicker to walk. And we were wedged in with sacks, parcels and produce of all descriptions, including livestock. The horse, whose name if I remember rightly was Sam, never moved faster than walking pace, and when we came, on our homeward journey, to Joyner's Hill, with its gradient of one in ten, we had to get out and walk. Sometimes we even had to push. (Ralph Whitlock, *A Family and a Village*, 1969.)

Emigrants boarding carriers' carts to journey to the coast

2

The watery road

Celebrations at the opening of the Glastonbury canal in 1832

A watery passage

AN act was obtained in 1767, to make a Canal between Birmingham and the coal delphs about Wednesbury. The necessary article of coal, before this act, was brought by land, at about thirteen shillings per ton, but now at 8s. 4d. It was common to see a train of carriages for miles, to the great destruction of the road, and the annoyance of travellers.

This duct is extended in the whole to about twenty-two miles in length, till it unites with what we may justly term the grand artery, or Staffordshire Canal; which crossing the island, communicates with Hull, Bristol, and Liverpool. The expence was about £70,000 divided into shares £140 each, of which no man can purchase more than ten, and which in 1782 sold for about £370 and in 1792 for £1170...

This watery passage, exclusive of loading the proprietors with wealth, tends greatly to the improvement of some branches of trade, by introducing heavy materials at a small expence, such as pig iron for the founderies, lime-stone, articles for the manufacture of brass and steel, also stone, brick, slate, timber, &c. It is happy for the world, that public interest is grafted upon private, and that both flourish together.

This grand work, like other productions of Birmingham birth, was rather hasty; the managers, not being able to find patience to worm round the hill at Smethwick, or cut through, have wisely travelled over it by the help of twelve locks, with six they mount the summit, and with six more descend to the former level; forgetting the great waste of water, and the small supply from the rivulets, and also the amazing loss of time in climbing this curious ladder, consisting of twelve liquid steps. These locks are now reduced in number...

The boats are nearly alike, constructed to fit the locks,

carry about twenty-five tons, and are each drawn by something like the skeleton of a horse, covered with skin; whether he subsists upon the scent of the water, is a doubt; but whether his life is a scene of affliction is not; for the unfeeling driver has no employment but to whip him from one end of the canal to the other. While the teams practised the turnpike road, the lash was divided among five unfortunate animals, but now the whole wrath of the driver falls upon one. We can scarcely view a boat travelling this liquid road, without raising opposite sensations – pleased to think of its great benefit to the community, and grieved to behold wanton punishment. (William Hutton, *An History of Birmingham to 1780*, 1782.)

Sailing to Croydon

On Monday last, the navigation of this Canal from the Thames to the town of Croydon was opened. The proprietors . . . met at Sydenham and there embarked on one of the company's barges, which was handsomely decorated with flags, &c. At the moment of this barge's moving forward an excellent band played 'God save the King', and a salute of 21 guns was fired. The proprietors' barge then advanced, followed by a great many barges, loaded some of them with coals, others with stone, corn &c, &c. . .

When the Proprietors approached the basin at Croydon, they saw it surrounded by many thousands of persons, assembled to greet, with thanks and applause, those by whose patriotic perseverance so important a work had been accomplished. It is impossible to describe, adequately, the scene which presented itself, and the feelings which prevailed, when the Proprietors' barge was entering the basin, at which instant the band was playing 'God Save the King', the guns were firing, the bells of the churches were ringing; and this immense concourse of delighted persons were hailing by universal and hearty, and long continued shouts, the dawn of their commerce and prosperity.

The following air, written by a Gentleman, while sailing to Croydon, was most zealously and ably sung by one of the Proprietors, Mr J. Walsh, and was received with great applause.

The Croydon Canal

1 All hail this grand day when with gay colours flying,
   The barges are seen on the current to glide,
   When with fond emulation all parties are vying,
   To make our Canal of Old England the pride.
   Long down its fair stream may the rich vessel glide,
   And the Croydon Canal be of England the pride.

2 And may it long flourish, while commerce caressing,
   Adorns its gay banks with her wealth-bringing stores;
   To Croydon, and all round the country a blessing,
   May industry's sons ever thrive on its shores!

3 And now my good fellows sure nothing is wanting
   To heighten our mirth and our blessings to crown,
   But with the gay belles on its banks to be flaunting,
   When spring smiles again on this high-favoured town.

(*The Times*, 27 October 1809.)

There is no specific tune indicated for this song but the words could be sung to a suitably nautical contemporary melody, such as *Spanish Ladies*.

Song 6 *Grantham Navigation*

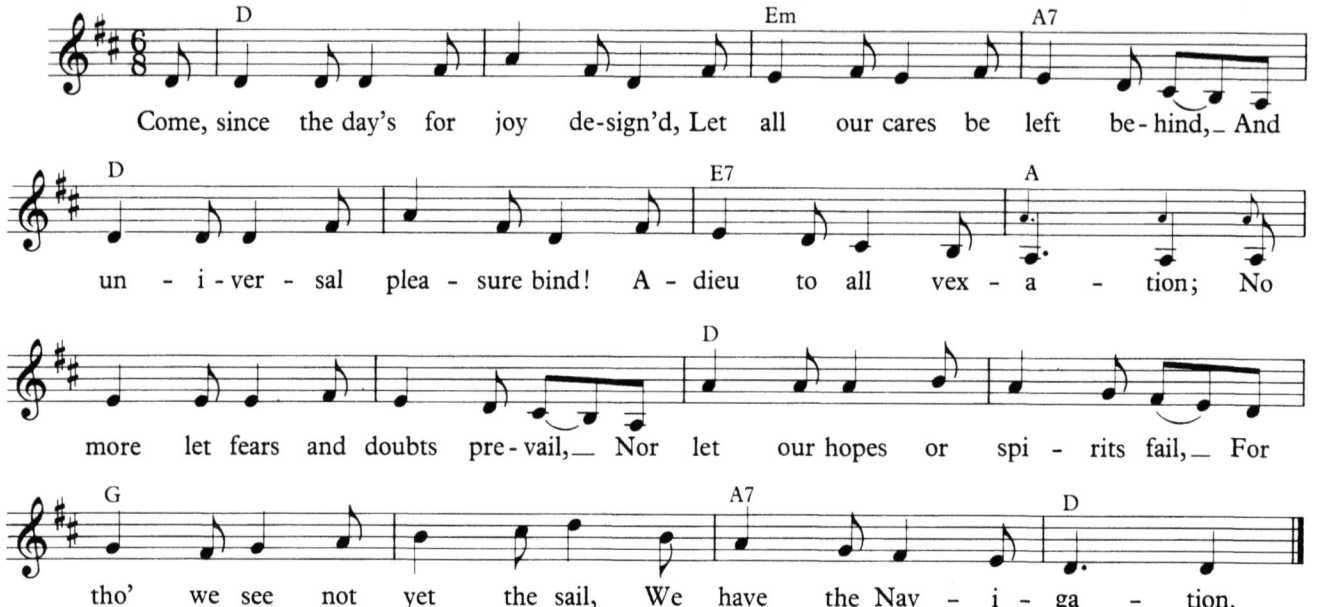

2 Let Thames, the Trent, the Severn too,
   Each stream which in the world doth flow,
   There various stores of traffic shew,
   With envious exultation;
   But now no more; their triumph vain,
   This inland borough will maintain
   Its fame, & still unrivall'd reign
   Secure by Navigation.

3 And thanks to Heav'n since 'tis perform'd,
   The poor will now be cloathed & warm'd,
   'Gainst wintry winds & tempest arm'd,
   Snug in their habitation;
   The old & young with equal joy
   Will raise their voices to the sky
   And children yet unborn will cry
   Bless'd Grantham Navigation.

4 The rising wharf we soon shall see,
   And commerce wide extended be,
   From inland Grantham to the sea,
   And far remotest nation;
   The freighted bark with merchandize,
   And hardy tars to steer the prize,
   Will oft returning glad our eyes,
   Thro' Grantham Navigation.

5 Thy lofty spire shall wondering tell,
   Recording History too shall spell
   To distant days thy fame, & swell
   The world with admiration;
   For long as *Granby's* name shall be
   To future ages told, you'll see
   This borough flourish great & free,
   And boast her Navigation.

6 The peopled streets will now increase,
   The town will smile, & trade ne'er cease,
   Tho' war be wag'd, or if at peace,
   We traffic thro' the nation;
   Who's then so blest, or so secure?
   We feed the hungry, cloath the poor,
   Of never ending commerce sure,
   By Grantham Navigation.

7 Let ev'ry heart true pleasure feel,
   On this occasion shew his zeal,
   His wishes for the public weal,
   Whatever be his station;
   Prepare his bumper, nor delay
   In chorus now to sing & say,
   Grantham for ever, & huzza
   To Grantham Navigation.

Grantham: in Lincolnshire. Granby: the reference is probably to the Marquess of Granby (1721-70) who gained fame by leading the British cavalry in a victorious charge against the French at the Battle of Warburg in 1760. The story goes that his wig flew off his head in the charge and that he shouted, 'We'll go for 'em baldheaded', thus coining a phrase. He was a son of the third Duke of Rutland, whose successors supported the plan for the Grantham Navigation.

After an unsuccessful attempt in 1792 a parliamentary act permitting the construction of a 30-mile canal from Grantham to Nottingham was passed in 1793, receiving the royal assent from George III on 30 April. Elated by the news, an anonymous 'Gentleman of Grantham' sat down and wrote a celebratory song and sent it off to his local newspaper, *The Stamford Mercury* (which still exists), where it appeared on 17 May. The song rhapsodically lists the anticipated benefits of the canal, which took four years to build, and opened in 1797. The writer's hopes seem to have been realised: a twentieth-century historian concludes that 'on the whole, the canal was of great benefit to the communities it served, and especially to the town of Grantham itself'.

No tune was indicated, but *Nancy Dawson* fits very well. This was popular at the time, and was used for at least one other canal song, John Freeth's *Inland Navigation*.

Canal bandits

In the making of canals, it is the general custom to employ gangs of hands who travel from one work to another and do nothing else. These banditti, known in some parts of England by the name of 'Navies' or 'Navigators', and in others by that of 'Bankers', are generally the terror of the surrounding country; they are as completely a class by themselves as the Gipsies. Possessed of all the daring recklessness of the Smuggler, without any of his redeeming qualities, their ferocious behaviour can only be equalled by the brutality of their language. It may be truly said, their hand is against every man, and before they have been long located, every man's hand is against them; and woe befal any woman, with the slightest share of modesty, whose ears they can assail.

From being long known to each other, they in general act in concert, and put at defiance any local constabulary force; consequently crimes of the most atrocious character are common, and robbery, without an attempt at concealment, has been an everyday occurrence, wherever they have been congregated in large numbers. (Peter Lecount, *The History of the Railways Connecting London and Birmingham*, 1839.)

Navvies building the Manchester Ship Canal in the late nineteenth century

Song 7 *Paddy upon the canal*

2. I being a poor Irish stranger,
   And knowing not what for to say,
   When the ganger came up in a hurry,
   Saying, 'Boys, it's a gay time of day',
   They all stood up in good order,
   You'd thought him father of all;
   I was wishing that very same moment
   I was dying upon the canal.

3. I fell in love with a farmer's daughter,
   And she was right proud, do you see?
   I caught her right round by the middle
   And set her right down on my knee.
   The old woman got up in a hurry
   And loudly began for to bawl,
   Saying, 'Get out, you jaucy big jade,
   For Paddy will prove your downfall.'

4. The girls they do all love me here,
   Or wherever that I do go:
   There's Sarah and Betsy and Polly,
   They all do call me their beau.
   The old woman got up in a hurry
   And loudly began for to bawl,
   Saying, 'We never got good of our daughter
   Since Paddy came on the canal.'

5. I learnt the art of navigation;
   I think it's a very fine trade:
   I can handle the pick and the shovel,
   Likewise the wheelbarrow and spade.
   I learned to be very handy;
   Although I am not very tall,
   I could handle the sprig of shillelagh
   With every a boy on the canal.

6 So now to conclude and to finish,
   And to publish in every degree,
   I'm just as true-hearted an Irishman
   As ever your country did see.
   So fill up a glass and be hearty
   And drink a good health to us all,
   And to every true-hearted Irishman
   That's digging upon the canal.

Ganger: foreman. The word first appeared in print, according to Partridge's *Dictionary of Historical Slang*, about 1849. This is therefore a very early reference, since it dates from 1847. Shillelagh: cudgel (pronounced 'shillayli').

   The song appeared as a printed sheet for sale in the streets. It has no printer's name. The original purchaser wrote at the bottom, 'Bought Newcastle Race Week 1847'.

A harsh apprenticeship
I was apprenticed early [probably at the age of 11 or 12, in 1830 or 1831] to one Toby Duffell, a gun-lock filer, and also a publican, living on the Leas, near the Ranters' Chapel, in Darlaston . . . One day my mistress gave me the remains of a pot of beef broth to give to the dogs. I set this down, without seeing that there was in it a piece of hard shin-bone. One of my master's best dogs seized this bit of bone, and was quietly gnawing it in a corner when its owner unfortunately came in, and fearing his pet's teeth would be destroyed, turned his fury upon me, and so beat me that I at once bolted, and, for the time, cut his acquaintance and lock-filing. Having made my escape, I wandered along The Leisures until I was lucky enough to obtain employment at half-a-crown [see page 10] a week on the fly-boat running to Worcester. My business was to take the shift either day or night in driving the towing horses. After some time I learned to steer the boat, and gave up the whip to another hand. In passing the locks it was my place to assist in opening and shutting the lock gates, and as I was deficient in strength for this purpose, my employer bestowed on me heavier curses, and still heavier blows. So fearfully was I beaten that I determined to take French leave of this freshwater sailing. Learning from a lad on the boat that, in a tunnel through which we had to pass for a distance of two miles, there was a sort of landing-place, I made up my mind to jump off the boat I was steering, unseen by the man who was 'legging' [see page 25] her through the tunnel.

   This I succeeded in doing, and at once made off, guiding myself through the slime and ooze by groping with my hands against the damp and dripping wall. After what seemed to me hours of crawling along I came to a flight of steps, up which I proceeded for some time. I at last saw a light ahead, but on reaching it found the stairway blocked by a heavy iron grating, which was locked. I shouted and screeched the remainder of the afternoon, till, completely worn out by cold, hunger and fatigue, I fell into a deep sleep, and never stirred till morning. Feeling then somewhat refreshed by my long rest, I began shouting again, endeavouring to draw the attention of some chance passer-by or inmate of the place, which I afterward found to be one of the underground entrances to Dudley Castle. At length a woman belonging to the castle passed by my prison bars on her way to find her cows, and, hearing my clamour, brought the blacksmith, who, after calling a constable, cut the lock from the grating, and so far released me. But this was merely out of the frying-pan into the fire; for on being questioned, and my account of myself not being satisfactory, I was marched off to the lock-up, and, upon inquiry being made, I was discovered to be a runaway apprentice from Darlaston, and forthwith handed over to my former employer of bull-dog-keeping fame. After being taken to him at Darlaston I was removed to Bilston, tried for my desertion, and sentenced to one month in Stafford Gaol, with a flogging at the beginning and the end of the term. After my last flogging and discharge I was so overcome with the fear of further punishment that I hastened back to the place of my apprenticeship, passing through Pancridge and Wolverhampton. (William Derricourt (or Day), *Old Convict Days*, 1899.)

Two passengers
A confused sound of voices, mingling with her dreams, awoke her. A man of very uncouth and rough appearance was standing over them [Little Nell and her grandfather], and two of his companions were looking on, from a long, heavy boat which had come close to the bank while they were sleeping. The boat had neither oar nor sail, but was towed by a couple of horses, who, with the rope to which they were harnessed slack and dripping in the water, were resting on the path.

   'Holloa!' said the man, roughly. 'What's the matter here?'
   'We were only asleep, sir,' said Nell. 'We have been walking all night.'

'A pair of queer travellers to be walking all night,' observed the man who had first accosted them. 'One of you is a trifle too old for that sort of work, and the other a trifle too young. Where are you going?'

Nell faltered, and pointed a hand towards the West, upon which the man inquired if she meant a certain town, which he named. Nell, to avoid more questioning, said, 'Yes, that was the place.' . . .

'You may go with us if you like,' replied one of those in the boat. 'We're going to the same place.' . . .

Before she had had any more time for consideration, she and her grandfather were on board, and gliding smoothly down the canal. The sun shone pleasantly on the bright water, which was sometimes shaded by trees, and sometimes open to a wide extent of country, intersected by running streams, and rich with wooded hills, cultivated land, and sheltered farms. Now and then, a village with its modest spire, thatched roofs, and gable-ends, would peep out from among the trees; and, more than once, a distant town, with great church towers looming through its smoke, and high factories or workshops rising above the mass of houses, would come in view, and, by the length of time it lingered in the distance, show them how slowly they travelled . . .

They had, for some time, been gradually approaching the place for which they were bound. The water had become thicker and dirtier; other barges, coming from it, passed them frequently; the paths of coal-ash and huts of staring brick marked the vicinity of some great manufacturing town; while scattered streets and houses, and smoke from distant furnaces, indicated that they were already in the outskirts. Now, the clustered roofs and piles of buildings trembling with the working of engines, and dimly resounding with their shrieks and throbbings; the tall chimneys vomiting forth a black vapour, which hung in a dense, ill-favoured cloud above the housetops, and filled the air with gloom; the clank of hammers beating upon iron, the roar of busy streets and noisy crowds, gradually augmenting until all the various sounds blended into one, and none was distinguishable for itself, announced the termination of their journey. (Charles Dickens, *The Old Curiosity Shop*, 1841, ch. 43.)

ON
Leeds Becoming A
SEA-PORT TOWN.

Copyright.

Oh dear! oh dear! this a curious age is,
Alteration all the rage is—
Young and old in the stream are moving
All in the general cry improving,
From the Exhibition I've brought news down, sirs,
They're going to make it a sea-port town sirs,
Then instead of Factories and cheap tailors,
Nothing you'll see but ships & sailors

CHORUS.

This 'twill be I'll bet you a crown sirs.
When Leeds it is a sea-port town sirs.

When the first ship appears in sight,
The town will all be joy & delight;
Eating, drinking, dancing, singing,
The old church spire will shake with ringing
Then we shall meet with touts and prigs, sirs,
Aldermen too in their gowns & wigs sirs,
The heads of the town with all their forces,
And the ——— new Mayor they'll draw with Horses.
Thus 'twill be, &c.

All over the town there'll be boats and barges,
Man-o'-war ships that never so large is;
Steamers backwards and forwards towing,
You'll ride for nothing, and they'll pay you for going,
Sailors swearing, spars a battering,
Heave-ye-hoing hand-spikes clattering,
Strange sails crowding every day, sirs,
Sailing & Anchoring in Leeds bay sirs
Thus 'twill be, &c.

The Liverpool Gents they'll all be undone,
Here there will be nought but fun done,
Pats half wild, running there rigs sirs
Landing their butter, their bullocks, and pigs, sirs,
Then to make us merry and frisky—
Mealy potatoes & barrels of Whiskey
New-laid eggs a twelve-month taken,
And old maids with money as rusty as bacon.
Thus 'twill be, &c.

Such lots of goods the boats will bring up,
Store-rooms will like mushrooms spring up;
To hold the wares of all nations
The town must have a transformation
They'll make the town-hall into a store-house,
News rooms they'll make out of the workhouse,
At Dock street, grocers will put their figs by,
And Vicars croft they'll make into a pigsty
Thus 'twill be, &c

In a short time you'll have trade enough, sirs,
All over the world you'll send your stuff, sirs,
Goods of every clime and nation,
Will all come here for embarkation,
Machinery & Cloth, Coals & Carrots,
In return they'll get Poll Parrots,
Baboons Racoons & spanish Donkeys
Jay's Cockatoos & ringtail'd Monkeys
Thus 'twill be, &c.

In a few years, say perhaps twenty,
Man-o'-war ships will arrive in plenty,
Then as the tide of time encroaches,
They'll run 'em about the street like coaches,
Over the Marshes, stones & Crosses,
Tars for Jarvies, Whales for Horses;
But I'll be off, first I'll make my bow sirs,
For, ecod, I believe there's a ship coming now, sirs,
Thus 'twill be, &c.

Exhibition: the Great Exhibition of 1851. Prigs: pickpockets. Liverpool Gents: shipping magnates. Pats: Irishmen. The reference is probably to emigrants who, instead of landing at Liverpool, would land at Leeds. Jarvies: hackney coachmen.

Other versions of this street ballad, with details suitably changed, refer to Birmingham and Manchester. One, entitled, *Seaport Town of* ———, allowed the singer to put in any town he thought fit. The Leeds and Liverpool Canal was opened in 1816, but it seems that the ballad is almost pure fantasy. It was printed in the 1840s or, as this version, in the early 1850s. The words of this version are from the Kidson Broadside Collection, Mitchell Library, Glasgow.

There is no indication of the tune to which it was sung. With some minor adaptation of the words *The Rakes of Mallow* would fit.

On the canal I

Ordinary tourists start from wharves near the Custom House, or Saint Katherine's Docks; old fashioned inn yards, or White Horse Cellars; large and noisy railway stations; and some from their own stables, with a dog-cart and a fast trotting mare. I was an extraordinary tourist, and my point of starting was a Basin. Goods, bales, boxes, casks and cases were the uniform rule at the company's station, and passengers a startling, and one in half-a-century exception. As we entered the large gas-lighted, roof-covered yard, amongst a group of Warwickshire, Staffordshire, and Lancashire bargemen, dressed in their short fustian trousers, heavy boots, red plush jackets, waistcoats with pearl buttons and fustian sleeves, and gay silk handkerchieves slung loosely round their necks, we were looked upon as unwarrantable intruders, until received and conducted to our bounding bark by the attentive manager. We threaded our way between waggons, horses, cranes, bales, and men, until we stood before the black pool of water that ran up from the basin under the company's buildings. Here upon its inky bosom was the long thin form of the fly-boat *Stourport*, commanded by Captain Randle, in which it had been arranged we should make our journey on the canals as far as Birmingham, or even beyond that town if we felt so disposed . . .

The *Stourport* may be taken as a fair specimen of the fly-boats which are now employed in the carrying trade upon the canals that intersect England in every direction, joining each other, and covering a length of nearly two thousand five hundred miles. For the conveyance of heavy goods that do not require a rapid transit, these boats still maintain, and are always likely to maintain their position, unaffected by railway competition; and it has been demonstrated that with the application of equal forces, canal carriage will move at the rate of two and a half miles an hour – (the average speed of the fly-boats) – a weight nearly four times as great as railway carriage, and more than three times as great as turnpike-road carriage. These fly-boats belong to various individuals, firms and companies scattered throughout the country; the largest owners being my worthy hosts, the Grand Junction Canal Company, who, in addition to being extensive canal proprietors, are also active carriers . . .

About one o'clock in the morning we reached the Islington tunnel, and here we are enlightened as to another process of barge propulsion, called legging. A couple of strong, thick boards, very like in shape to tailors' sleeve boards, but twice the size, are hooked on to places formed on each side of the barge, near the head, from which they project like two raised oars. On these two narrow, insecure platforms, the two venturesome boatmen lie on their backs, holding on by grasping the board underneath, and with their legs up to the waist hanging over the water. A lantern, placed at the head of the barge, serves to light the operation which consists in moving the *Stourport* through the black tunnel by a measured side-step against the slimy, glistening walls; the right foot is first planted in a half-slanting direction, and the left foot is constantly brought over with a sweep to take the vacated place, until the right can recover its footing. The *Stourport*, steered by its commander, Captain Randle, walks through the tunnel in the dead of night by the aid of its four stout legs and its four heavily hob-nailed boots that make a full echoing sound upon the walls like the measured clapping of hands but disturb not the sleeping inmates of houses and kitchens under which they pass; many of whom, perhaps, are ignorant of the black and barge-loaded Styx that flows beneath them.

We emerge from the tunnel, at last, and tackle to our horse. Our progress is then slow and steady between the silent houses of Camden Town; past the anything but silent railway carrying establishment of the Messrs Pickford; round the outskirts of Regent's Park; under the overhanging trees of the Zoological Gardens; and through Saint John's Wood, to the termination of the Regent's Canal, and the commencement of the Grand Junction Canal, near the Harrow Road, at Paddington. About this time my friend and companion, Cuddy, who is remarkable for an appetite that requires satisfying at the most extraordinary times and seasons, could be restrained no longer from attacking the great meat-pie. A large watchman's lantern was handed down the hold; and, by its rather dim light, at exactly two A.M., the frugal meal began. (John Hollingshead, in *Household Words*, 11 September 1858.)

The Leeds canal

Song 8   *The cruise of the 'Calabar'*

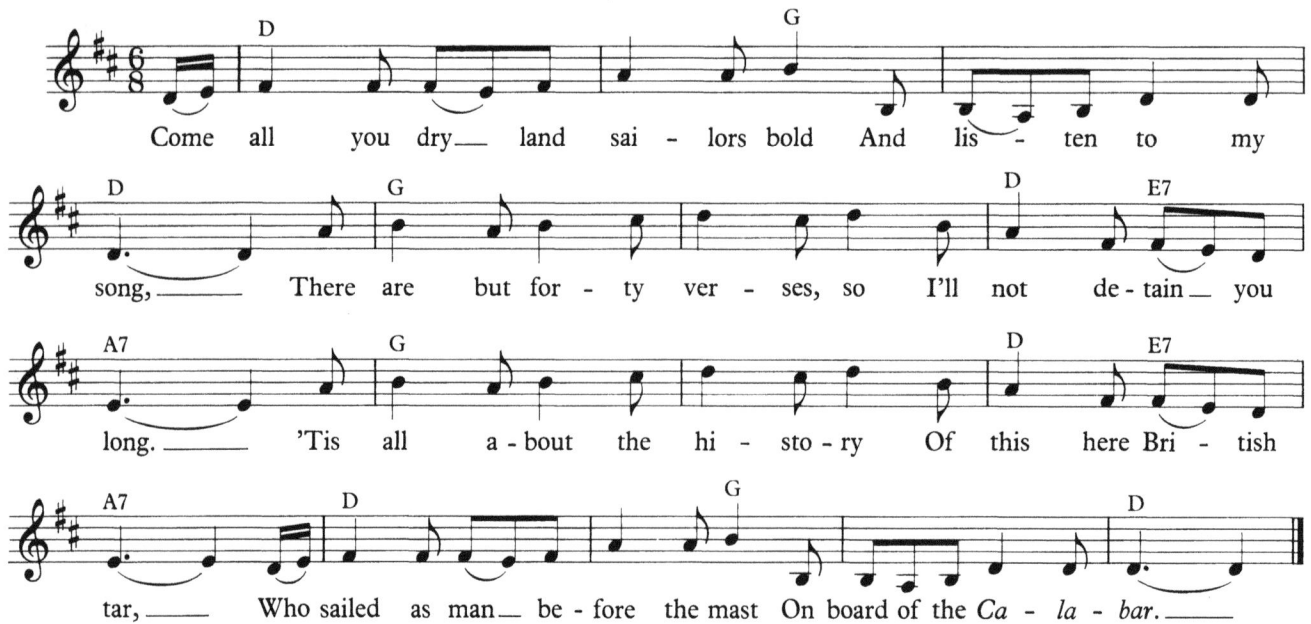

2 The *Calabar* was a clipper flat,
    Copper fastened fore and aft;
    The rudder stuck away out behind,
    The wheel was a great big shaft,
    With half a gale to swell each sail
    She made ten knots an hour,
    Being the smartest craft on the canal,
    Tho' only one horse power.

3 Our vessel ploughed the waters of
    The Liverpool Canal,
    Being under close reefed topsails,
    The glass foretold a squall.
    'Twas in Oldhall-street basin where
    We beat about in the surf,
    Bound for the Port of Sandhills Bridge.
    With a cargo of Irish turf.

4 Our Captain was a strapping youth,
    His height was four feet two,
    His eyes were black, his nose was red,
    His cheeks a Prussian blue.
    He wore a leather medal that
    He won in the Crimean War;
    His wife was Pilot and passenger's cook
    On board the *Calabar*.

5 We started with a favouring breeze,
    The weather being sublime;
    But just in the Straits of Burlington Bridge,
    Where two can't pass at a time;
    We were struck amidships by another flat,
    That gave us a serious check,
    She stove in our larboard paddle-box
    And destroyed our hurricane deck.

6 Now all became confusion, while
    The stormy winds did blow,
    Our bos'un slipped on an orange peel
    And fell in the hold below.
    The Captain said, press on all speed
    For on us she does gain,
    The next time I'm bound for Wigan, boys,
    By jabers, I'll go by train.

7 We got our arms all ready, boys,
    To meet the coming foe,
    Our grappling irons and boarding pikes,
    And Armstrong guns also
    Turn on full speed, the Captain cried,
    For we were sorely press'd.
    Our engineer cried from the bank,
    The horse is doing his best.

8 Oh! think how fast the heroes fell,
  In torrents the blood was spilt,
  Numbers falling before they were touched,
  To make sure they wouldn't be kilt.
  When the enemy struck up her flag,
  Our crew were laid on their backs,
  We found that she was a sister flat,
  With a cargo of cobbler's wax.

9 While huddling ashore near Athol Bridge –
  A very dangerous part –
  We ran bow on to a cob of coal,
  That wasn't marked on the chart.
  To keep our vessel from sinking, and
  To save each precious life,
  We threw the cargo overboard,
  Including the Captain's wife.

10 I've told you how the Captain's wife
   Was thrown in the briny deep;
   She haunts our vessel every night,
   And the devil a wink we sleep.
   Her spirit, dressed in mourning, boys,
   Along the deck does trot,
   The only thing that lays her ghost,
   Is a noggin of gin made hot.

Flat: canal boat. Great big shaft: the tiller. Ten knots an hour: both incorrect terminology (a knot is a speed of one nautical mile per hour) and a gross exaggeration; but the intention of the song is not to be exact. The Liverpool Canal: from Liverpool to Leeds, constructed between 1770 and 1777 (as far as Shipley) and 1790 and 1816 (from Shipley to Leeds). Oldhall-street basin, Sandhills Bridge, Burlington Bridge: all in Liverpool. Crimean War: ended in 1856. Larboard: port (left-hand) side. Armstrong guns: improved model of field gun used during the Crimean War and afterwards. Athol Bridge: again in Liverpool.

The *Liverpool Guide* of 1796 (reprinted by the City of Liverpool, 1974) mentions 'the head of the Leeds and Wigan canal', near St Paul's Church, and adds: 'an elegant Packet boat passes from hence to Wigan, every morning (except Sunday) at eight, and arrives there at six o'clock; and another from thence sets off at six, and arrives here at four. The Fares; 3s. and 2s. (see page 10). The right bank of the Canal affords a very pleasant walk; but is inaccessible, from dirt and the parsimony of the Proprietors, in wet weather; and there is no carriageway. The quantity of Coal imported by this canal, from Wigan, &c. for the supply of the town, and the export to the different parts of Europe, America and the West Indies, is considerable' (p. 59).

The song is widely known in Ireland and the North of England, often with local variations on the place names, though the name of the vessel varies only in its spelling. Our version was 'sung by Billy Richardson for many years at Sam Hagues, St James's Hall, Liverpool', to the tune of *Limerick Town is beautiful*. I have not been able to identify Billy Richardson, but from the references to the Crimean War it seems reasonable to argue that he was performing in the late 1850s.

By this time the earlier mood of elation at the technical triumphs of canals had given way to a mocking humour which used the terminology of deep sea sailing ironically.

On the canal II
As the morning developed, the promise of a fine day was fulfilled; and after we passed the brick-kiln country near Brentford, we proceeded in a zig-zag direction towards Uxbridge and Rickmansworth. The further we went the more our long-cherished notions of the dry, utilitarian character of canals disappear, to give place to a feeling of admiration for the picturesque beauty of the country and the artificial river, lying and running unheeded so near the metropolis. Reclining here and there upon the rich grass banks, or standing solitary, or in groups of three or four upon the towing path, were patient anglers, all having the stamp of dwellers in the closest portion of the metropolis . . .

Our horses are as docile, intelligent and well behaved as the trained steeds of the circus; and for many miles they are left to go on unled, chewing their provender in their milking-can nose-bags . . . At bridges where the towing path does not pass under the arch the mere unhooking of the rope is sufficient, and the horse, freed from the weight of the barge, walks quickly up the incline over the bridge and down to the path, even when, as is frequently the case, it changes to the other side of the canal. There he patiently waits until his burden floats through and the rope is hooked on again.

The Grand Junction Canal, passing in a zig-zag direction through parts of Middlesex, Hertfordshire, Bedfordshire, Buckinghamshire, to Braunston in Northamptonshire, is about forty-three feet in surface breadth, upwards of ninety miles in length, and, with one or two falls, is on a gradual rise from Paddington. The locks are expensive structures, costing, when double, two thousand pounds apiece; and many of them are so close together that they form a series of steps in a waterfall staircase . . .

The *Stourport* is rather faded in its decorations, and is not a gay specimen of the fly-barge in all its glory of cabin paint and varnish; but still enough remains to show what it was in its younger days, and what it will be again when it gets a week in dock for repairs at Birmingham. The boatman lavishes all his taste: all his rude, uncultivated love for the fine arts upon the external and internal ornaments of his floating home. His chosen colours are red, yellow and blue: all so bright that, when newly laid on and appearing under the rays of a mid-day sun, they are too much for the unprotected eye of the unaccustomed stranger. The two sides of the cabin, seen from the bank and the towing path, present a couple of landscapes in which there is a lake, a castle, a sailing-boat, and a range of mountains, painted after the great teaboard school of art.

Small as the *Stourport* cabin is for four full-grown boatmen, cabins just as small are made to accommodate large families that spring up among the river population. The Grand Junction Canal Company do not allow any of their barges to be turned into what are called family-boats; but amongst the small proprietors there is no such restriction; while the slow-boats, or boats that only travel during the day, resting at night, because they are towed without a change of horses, belong in most cases to the men who conduct them, and who, of course, are free to act as they think proper. The way this freedom is exercised is shown by the pictures of family-barges and their internal economy which pass us at every turn. There is the boatman, and his wife, a stout, sunburnt woman; and children, varying in number from two to ten, and in ages from three weeks to twelve years . . . When these helpless creatures reach five or six years of age they are entrusted with a whip and made useful to their thoughtless parents by night and day as drivers of the horse that tows the boat . . .

The boatmen were preparing for the passage of the Blisworth tunnel (nearly two miles in length) an underground journey of an hour's duration. At the mouth of the tunnel were a large number of leggers, waiting to be employed; their charge being one shilling to leg the boat through. We engaged one of these labourers for our boat to divide the duty with one of our boatmen; while the youth went overland with the horse . . . To beguile the tedium of the slow, dark journey – to amuse the leggers whose work is fearfully hard and acts upon the breath after the first quarter of a mile; and above all to avail themselves of the atmospheric effects of the tunnel; the boatmen at the tillers nearly all sing, and our vocalist was the captain's son.

If any observer will take the trouble to examine the character of the songs that obtain the greatest popularity amongst men and women engaged in heavy and laborious employments, he will find that the ruling favourite is the plaintive ballad. Comic songs are hardly known. The main secret of the wide popularity of the ballad lies in the fact that it generally contains a story, and is written in a measure that fits easily into a slow, drawling, breath-taking tune which all the lower orders know; and which – so far as I can find – has never been written or printed on paper; but has been handed down from father or mother to son and daughter, from generation to generation, from the remotest times. The plots of these ballad stories are generally based upon the passion of love; love of the most hopeless and melancholy kind; and the suicide of the heroine, by drowning in a river, is a poetical occurrence as common as jealousy.

There may have been a dozen of these ballads chanted in the Blisworth tunnel at the same time. The wail of our straw-haired singer rising, to our ears, above the rest. They came upon our ears, mixed with the splashing of water, in drowsy cadence, and at long intervals, like the moaning of a maniac chained to a wall. The effect upon the mind was, in this dark passage, to create a wholesome belief in the existence of large masses of misery and the utter nothingness of the things of the upper world. (John Hollingshead, in *Household Words*, 18 and 25 September 1858.)

A wedding
The banns having been published and no impediment alleged, the boat or barge having been securely hitched up to the canal side, the wedding-party made their way to the

parish church not many yards away. Now, the bargees have a style of their own, for they are to this day a people apart, and there is something so fascinating about them. The bride on this occasion was a tall, fair-haired young woman with bright blue eyes. Her dress, if not in the latest fashion, was much more modest than is generally seen to-day . . .

The bridegroom and his best man wore light blue dungarees, which had been specially washed, and so were now pale green. It was a great wedding. But it was the bride's mother who quite completed the sketch, which I have always regretted I did not have photographed. She appeared in a dress, coat and hat of twenty years previously! I could remember that style of dress, with its frills and flounces, and I liked the large broad hat, with its elongated feathers. It all took one back so vividly to the happy days before the war. There was an old-world touch about it . . .

Having sorted out the company and put all in order, the service proceeded with deep reverence, for when the bargees come to church they sometimes make curious mistakes, but they are always reverent and quite respectful. They are people of juvenile mind. When addressing the newly-married couple, as all the party stood at the Communion rails, it seemed strange – if supremely homely – to hear first one and then another ejaculate: 'Yes, mister.' 'Quite right, sir.' 'You never said a truer word, mister.'

And so the wedding passes off. On arrival at the vestry it is a common thing to discover that three out of the necessary four cannot sign their own names. At my first wedding, I remember asking the bridegroom about his occupation, and was on the point of writing him down as 'bargee', 'No, sir,' shouted half a dozen voices in chorus, 'not bargees – we are boatmen.' I apologised for my ignorance, and we parted, as we always do, on the best of terms. (F. G. Llewellin, *The Lighter Side of a Parson's Life*, n.d.)

Two canal boats waiting for the level in the locks to rise. An early nineteenth-century drawing

3

The iron road

Nine days' wonder?

A good many years ago, one of the toughest and hardest riders that ever crossed Leicestershire undertook to perform a feat which, just for the moment, attracted the general attention not only of the country but of the sporting world. His bet was that, if he might choose his own turf, and if he might select as many thoroughbred horses as he liked, he would undertake to ride 200 miles in ten hours.

The newspapers of the day described exactly how 'the Squire' was dressed – what he had been living on – how he looked – how, at the word 'Away!' he started like an arrow from a bow – how gallantly Tranby, his favourite racer, stretched himself in his gallop – how, on arriving at his second horse, he vaulted from one saddle to another – how he then flew over the surface of the earth, if possible, faster than before – and how, to the astonishment and amidst the acclamations of thousands of spectators, he at last came in ... a winner.*

Now, if at this moment of his victory, while with dust and perspiration on his brow – his exhausted arms dangling just above the panting flanks of his horse, which his friends at each side of the bridle were slowly leading in triumph – a decrepit old woman had hobbled forward, and in the name of Science had told the assembled multitude that before she became a skeleton she and her husband would undertake, instead of 200 miles in 10 hours, to go 500 – that is to say, for every mile 'the Squire' had just ridden, she and her old man would go two miles and a half – that she would moreover knit all the way, and that he should take his medicine every hour and read to her just as if they were at home; lastly, that they would undertake to perform their feat either in darkness or in daylight, in sunshine or in storm, 'in thunder, lightning, or in rain'; – who, we ask, would have listened to the poor maniac? – and yet how wonderfully would her prediction have been fulfilled. Nay, waggons of coals and heavy luggage nowadays fly across Leicestershire faster and farther than Mr Osbaldeston could go, notwithstanding his condition and that of all his horses.

When railways were first established, every living being gazed at a passing train with astonishment and fear: ploughmen held their breath; the loose horse galloped from it, and then, suddenly stopping, turned round, stared at it, and at last snorted aloud. But the 'nine days' wonder' soon came to an end. (Sir Francis Bond Head, *Stokers and Pokers*, 1849.)

The railway comes to Stagg's Gardens

The first shock of a great earthquake had, just at that period, rent the whole neighbourhood to its centre. Traces of its course were visible on every side. Houses were knocked down; streets broken through and stopped; deep pits and trenches dug in the ground: enormous heaps of earth and clay thrown up; buildings that were undermined and shaking, propped by great beams of wood. Here, a chaos of carts, overthrown and jumbled together, lay topsy-turvy at the bottom of a steep unnatural hill; there, confused treasures of iron soaked and rusted in something that had accidentally become a pond. Everywhere were bridges that led nowhere; thoroughfares that were wholly impassable; Babel towers of chimneys, wanting half their height; temporary wooden houses and enclosures, in the most unlikely situations; carcasses of ragged tenements, and fragments of unfinished walls and arches, and piles of scaffolding, and wildernesses of bricks, and giant forms of cranes, and tripods straddling above nothing. There were a hundred thousand shapes and substances of incompleteness, wildly mingled out of their places, upside down, burrowing in the earth, aspiring in the air, mouldering to the water, and unintelligible as any dream. Hot springs and fiery eruptions, the usual attendants upon earthquakes, lent their contributions of confusion to the scene. Boiling water hissed and heaved within dilapidated walls; whence, also the glare and roar of flames came issuing forth; and mounds of ashes blocked up rights of way, and wholly changed the law and custom of the neighbourhood. In short, the yet unfinished and unopened Railroad was in progress; and, from the very core of all this dire disorder, trailed smoothly away, upon its mighty course of civilisation and improvement. (Charles Dickens, *Dombey and Son*, 1848, ch. 6; see also ch. 15. The extract refers to work in North London on the London to Birmingham line, which was started in 1835.)

On the Liverpool and Manchester

Liverpool, 10 June [1833] – At twelve I got upon an omnibus and was driven up a steep hill to the place where the steam-carriages start. We travelled in the second class of carriages. There were five carriages linked together, in each of which were placed open seats for the traveller, four and four facing each other; but not all were full; and, besides, there was a close carriage, and also a machine for luggage. The fare was four shillings for the thirty-one miles. Everything went

---

*The ride, by Squire Osbaldeston, took place at Newmarket in 1831. At the age of 54, the rider covered 200 miles in eight hours, 42 minutes (including the time for changes of mount and refreshments). See E. D. Cuming (ed.), *Squire Osbaldeston: His Autobiography* (1926).

on so rapidly that I had scarcely the power of observation. The road begins at an excavation through rock, and is to a certain extent insulated from the adjacent country. It is occasionally placed on bridges, and frequently intersected by ordinary roads. Not quite a perfect level is preserved. On setting off there is a slight jolt, arising from the chain catching each carriage, but, once in motion, we proceeded as smoothly as possible. For a minute or two the pace is gentle, and is constantly varying. The machine produces little smoke or steam. First in order is the tall chimney; then the boiler, a barrel-like vessel; then an oblong reservoir of water; then a vehicle for coals; and then comes, of a length infinitely extendible, the train of carriages. If all the seats had been filled, our train would have carried about 150 passengers; but a gentleman assured me at Chester that he went with a thousand persons to Newton fair. There must have been two engines then. I have heard since that two thousand persons and more went to and from the fair that day. But two thousand only, at three shillings each way, would have produced £600! But after all, the expense is so great that it is considered uncertain whether the establishment will ultimately remunerate the proprietors. Yet I have heard that it already yields the shareholders a dividend of nine per cent. And Bills have passed for making railroads between London and Birmingham, and Birmingham and Liverpool. What a change will it produce in the intercourse! One conveyance will take between 100 and 200 passengers, and the journey will be made in a forenoon! Of the rapidity of the journey I had bitter experience on my return; but I may say now that, stoppages included, it may certainly be made at the rate of twenty miles an hour!

I should have observed before that the most remarkable movements of the journey are those in which trains pass one another. The rapidity is such that there is no recognizing the features of a traveller. On several occasions the noise of the passing engine was like the whizzing of a rocket. Guards are stationed in the road, holding flags, to give notice to the drivers when to stop. (Henry Crabb Robinson, *Diary*, 1872.)

The opening of the Stockton and Darlington Railway in 1825

Song 9 *Newcastle and Carlisle railway*

2 The grand locomotives from Newcastle came,
How quick is their speed and how great is their fame;
The *Comet* so brilliant, she could not well lead,
For *Rapid* came in with abundance of speed.
The air it did ring with the cry of 'hurray',
When they came for to open the Carlisle Railway.

3 The hills were all clad on the south side of Tyne
To view the procession along the new line;
The drums they did beat and the colours did fly,
To cheer the spectators as they all passed by.
The men will rejoice and the women will pray
For all that subscribe to Newcastle Railway.

4 The masons they are the first workmen in town,
And some by hard labour can earn a full crown;
The blacksmiths and joiners all work to their plan,
And I scarcely can tell you who is the best man.
Let none of these workmen have reason to say
That they cannot live by the Carlisle Railway.

5 There is Squire Beaumont, for the sake of his heirs,
Oh it is well known that he holds fifty shares;
Full long may he live with his own darling son,
So let us all praise him for what he has done.
He will hear the birds sing in the sweet month of May
When he travels along on Newcastle Railway.

6 There is Mr Blackmoor, a worthy young man,
 To forward this line he will do all he can;
 In two or three years he will finish it well
 And make a through passage into the canal.
 So long may he live and still carry the sway,
 And set out more work on the Carlisle Railway.

7 When you see the steam coaches and all things complete,
 For four or five shillings you may take a seat;
 You may dine at Newcastle and then take your flight,
 And sup at Carlisle on the very same night.
 The new *Expedition* she will not delay
 As long as she runs on Newcastle Railway.

8 The cannons were planted upon the low ground;
 They made all the valleys to ring with their sound.
 The drums they did beat and the music did play
 Before they went back to Newcastle that day.
 Both the young and the old may remember that day,
 When they all drank success to Carlisle Railway.

9 When you see the waggons move on at full speed,
 Well laden with liquor, provisions and lead,
 You may fill up a glass of good rum or strong beer,
 And then drink a health to the head engineer.
 I hope he will live to see that happy day
 When they have completed Newcastle Railway.

Mr Blackmoor: John Blackmore, the railway engineer. Blackmore provided technical details for J. W. Carmichael's *Views on the Newcastle and Carlisle Railway* (1836-8). Dine at Newcastle and ... sup at Carlisle: not in fact possible until 1846.

'Many early railways followed the courses of canals which had been proposed but not carried out. The Canterbury and Whitstable had been one. The eighteen-twenties had seen proposals for something more substantial, a canal to connect Tyne and Solway. In place of this there was proposed an unusually ambitious railway, indeed the first to offer coast-to-coast connection. After four years of struggle, the Newcastle and Carlisle Railway, the first line across England, got its Act in May, 1829. It was to consist of a main line with branches to Alston and Swalwell, giving a total route mileage of 78½. Originally proposed for horse traction, a special Act had to be obtained to permit the substitution of steam. This did not come about until the opening of the first section, from Blaydon to Hexham (16¾ miles). Two locomotives, *Comet* and *Rapid*, were nevertheless unlawfully used from the opening on March 9, 1835. One Charles Bacon and his son got an injunction against the company, and the regular opening did not take place until May 9, after the Bacons had bowed to public protest. Construction went on section by section, at the western as well as the eastern end. The eleven miles from Greenhead to Haydon Bridge, opened on June 18, 1838, joined the eastern and western sections, but the eastern extremity from Blaydon to Newcastle (Forth) was not opened until May 21, 1839, and the Alston Branch from Haltwhistle (auspicious name!) was not opened until 1857, seven years after the extension of the eastern terminus from Forth to the new great Newcastle Central Station of the York, Newcastle and Berwick Railway.

'The Newcastle and Carlisle Railway got a monopoly of the traffic in iron ore from north-western Cumberland to the East Coast, and during the 28 years of its independent existence, it steadily paid four to six per cent. on the Ordinary stock. Engineering features were on quite a grand scale, with large viaducts at Wetheral and Corby, the former, over the Eden, having five 80 ft. arches and a height of over 100 ft. Like other early railways, much of it was originally laid with fishbelly rails on stone blocks. The standard 4 ft. 8½ in. gauge was used, but for a long time the trains ran on the right-hand side' (Hamilton Ellis, *British Railway History*, vol. I, *1830-1876*, 1954, pp. 43-4).

Railways in their infancy

RAILWAYS were in their infancy when I was a small boy. An amazing development has taken place since then. The discomforts of travelling were very great in those early days as compared with the present luxurious manner of locomotion. . . .

The carriages themselves were such that people in these days would hesitate to travel in them, at least in all those below the firsts, which were pretty much the same as now save for the lighting, heating, and height. The second classes were closed up to the top, but there were no cushions whatever either on the seats or backs. The thirds were not much inferior to the seconds, only that the divisions of the compartments did not extend much higher than the shoulders of the passengers when seated; so that you could see the heads of the travellers through the entire length of the carriage. Then there were carriages which were more like cattle trucks than anything else. These had no tops, and no divisions, but only a few seats or benches to sit upon. These we used to call 'fourths', though I do not think they were so designated by the companies. They were only endurable in summer weather. If it rained, you got drenched, unless you had a mackintosh; if it blew, as it invariably did, owing to the pace of the train, your hat had to be securely fastened, else you would probably lose it. I have a distinct recollection of travelling occasionally in these enormities, but only for short distances . . .

Then, as now, the great book of railway reference was *Bradshaw's Railway Guide*, first published in 1839, under the title of *Bradshaw's Railway Time Tables*. Although published at sixpence, a copy of the first edition is now quite a valuable possession. There was, however, an earlier publication of the kind, even than Bradshaw; this was called *Fowler's Railway Traveller's Guide*, published in Leeds in 1838. This publication I have had an opportunity of examining, and in the light of modern railway developments it is full of interest. Then, as a rule, only one third-class train was run each way in the day, and that generally early in the morning. The third-class carriages were frequently attached to goods trains, and the tedium of journeys under such conditions was very great; so that those who could afford it were practically compelled to travel first or second class. Various 'Instructions' are given in this *Guide* to travellers, one of which runs thus: 'Third Class Train; Passengers should fasten their hats by a ribbon to prevent them being blown off.' Again we read: 'To prevent accidents, passengers are warned to keep their seats when the trains are starting, going, or stopping, and invariably to get in and out of the left side of the carriages lest they should be knocked down by a passing train.' The admission of dogs into the carriages has been disallowed from the earliest days. Passengers were requested to attend to their own luggage, and to see that the porters and guards 'do place it in and upon the carriages' . . .

The landed gentry, generally speaking, had the greatest antipathy to railways, and would not have them near their property if they could help it. Many refused altogether at first to travel by rail, but by degrees some made a sort of compromise, and had their own private carriages placed on carriage trucks, and sat in them, at the end of the train, as though they were going out for a drive . . .

I can remember the excitement caused by the Great Exhibition of 1851. That was the first one of the kind. Thousands from Yorkshire went to see it who had never before in their lives been to London, and many of them not far from their homes. The competition between the railway companies in running cheap trips to see the Great Exhibition was so keen that at one time one could travel from York to London and back for five shillings, and crowds of people availed themselves of this opportunity of visiting the metropolis. (M. C. F. Morris, *Yorkshire Reminiscences*, 1922.)

London to Liverpool

Knowsley, 18 July [1838] – Tired of doing nothing in London, and of hearing about the Queen and the elections, I resolved to vary the scene and run down here to see the Birmingham railroad, Liverpool, and Liverpool races. So I started at five o'clock on Sunday evening, got to Birmingham at half-past five on Monday morning, and got upon the railroad at half-past seven. Nothing can be more comfortable than the vehicle in which I was put, a sort of chariot with two places, and there is nothing disagreeable about it but the occasional whiffs of stinking air which it is impossible to exclude altogether. The first sensation is a slight degree of nervousness and a feeling of being run away with, but a sense of security soon supervenes, and the velocity is delightful. Town after town, one park and *château* after another, are left behind with the rapid variety of a moving panorama, and the continual bustle and animation of the changes and stoppages make the journey very entertaining. The train was very long, and heads were continually popping out of the several carriages, attracted by well-known voices, and then came the greetings and exclamations of surprise, the 'Where are you going?' and 'How on earth came you here?' Considering the novelty of its establishment, there is very little embarrassment, and it certainly renders all other travelling irksome and tedious by comparison. It was peculiarly gay at this time, because there was so much going on. There were all sorts of people going to Liverpool races, barristers to the assizes, and candidates to their several elections. The day was so wet that I could not see the town of Liverpool. (Charles Greville, *Memoirs*, 1896.)

The duties of an engine-driver

THE DUTIES which the engine-driver has to perform are not only of vital importance, but of a nature which peculiarly illustrates the calm, unpretending, bull-dog courage, indigenous to the moist healthy climate of the British Isles. Even in bright sunshine, to stand – like the figure-head of a ship – foremost on a train of enormous weight, which, with fearful momentum, is rushing forward faster than any racehorse can gallop, requires a cool head and a calm heart; but to proceed at this pace in dark or foggy weather into tunnels, along embankments, and through deep cuttings, where it is impossible to foresee any obstruction, is an amount of responsibility which scarcely any other situation in life can exceed; for not only is a driver severely, and occasionally without mercy, punished for any negligence he himself may commit, but he is invariably sentenced personally to suffer on the spot for any accident that from the negligence of others may suddenly befall the road along which he travels, but over which he has not the smallest control. The greatest hardship he has to endure, however, is from cold, especially that produced in winter by evaporation from his drenched clothes passing rapidly through the air. Indeed, when a gale of wind and rain from the north-west, triumphantly sweeping over the surface of the earth at its ordinary rate of say sixty miles an hour, suddenly meets the driver of the London and North Western, who has not only to withstand such an antagonist, but to dash through him, and in spite of him to proceed in an opposite direction at the rate of say forty miles an hour – the conflict between the wet Englishman and Æolus, tilting by each other at the combined speed of a hundred miles an hour, forms a tournament of extraordinary interest.

As the engine is proceeding, the driver, who has not very many inches of standing-room, remains upon its narrow platform, while his fireman, on about the same space, stands close beside him on the tender. We tried the position. Everything, however, proved to be so hard, excepting the engine, which was both hard and hot, that we found it necessary to travel with one foot on the tender and the other on the engine, and, as the motion of each was very different, we felt as if each leg were galloping at a different stride. Nevertheless the Company's drivers and firemen usually travel from 100 to 120 miles per day, performing six of these trips per week; nay, a few run 166 miles per day – for which they are paid eight days' wages for six trips. (Sir Francis Bond Head, *Stokers and Pokers*, 1849.)

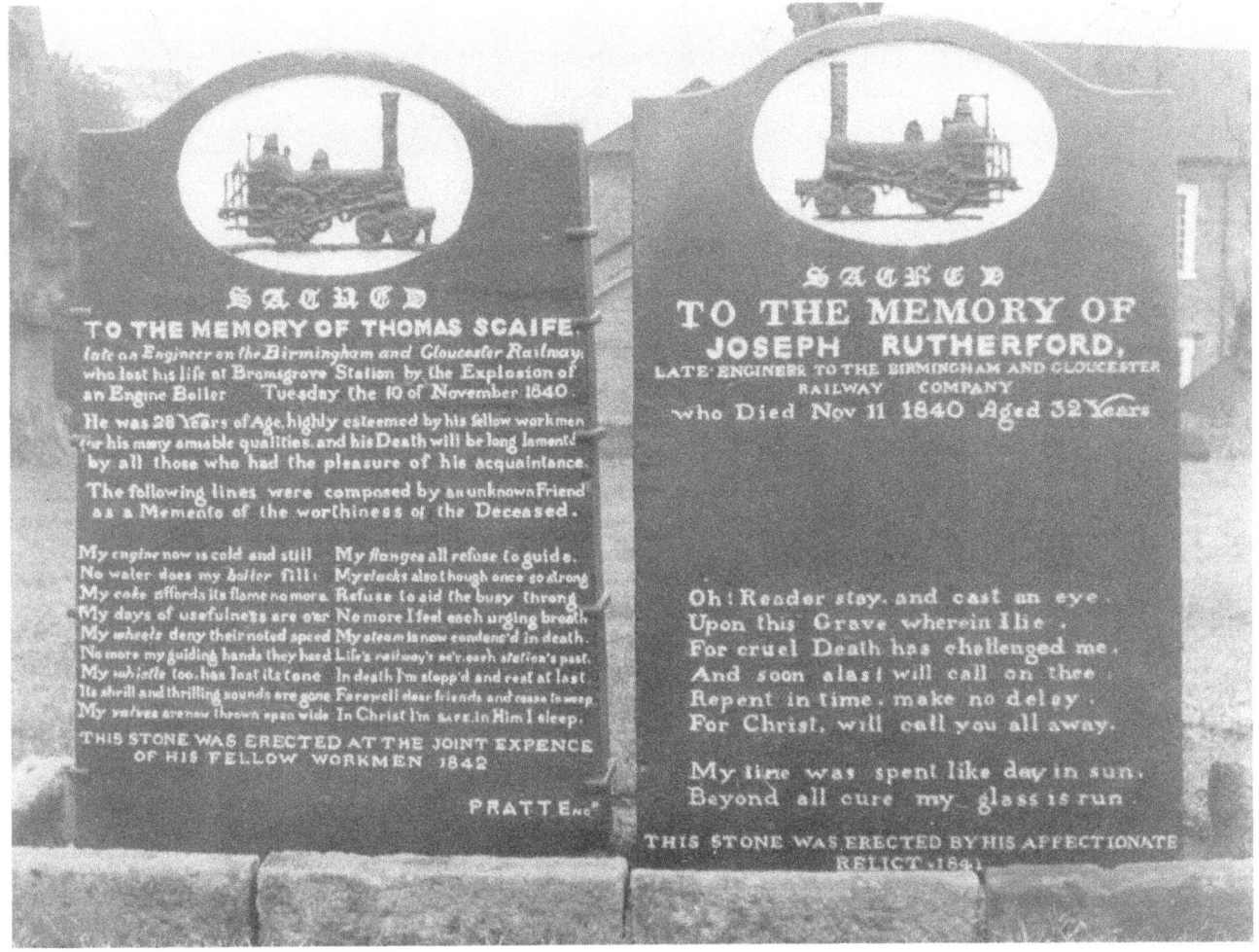

Headstones in Bromsgrove churchyard, commemorating the death of two engineers in a boiler explosion in 1840

Song 10 *The Great Western railroad, or, The pleasures of travelling by steam*

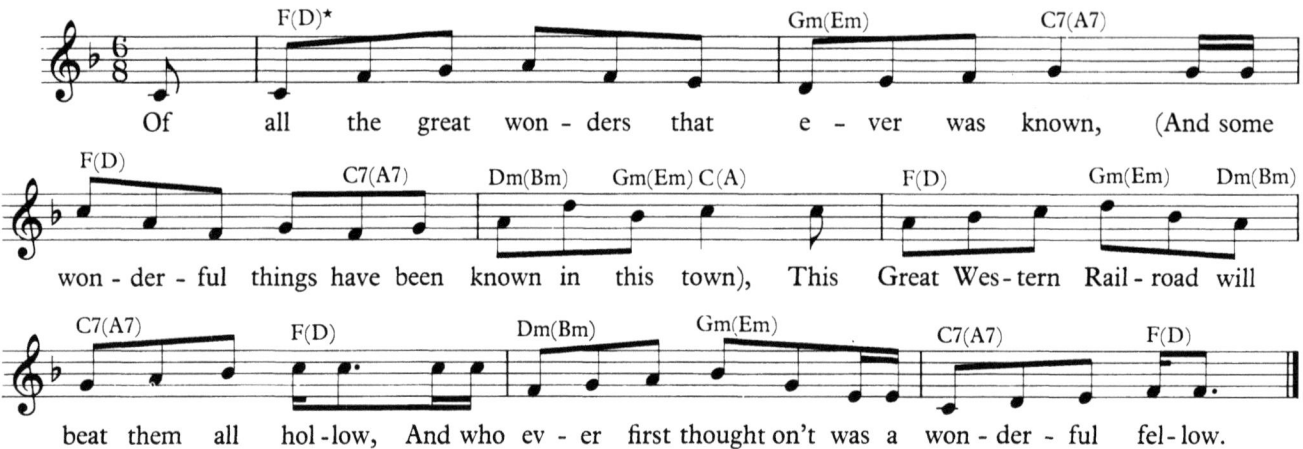

*Easier fingerings for these chords may be obtained by playing the alternatives shown in brackets, with capo on fret 3.

2 It's said when 'tis finished, which'll be in two years,
   If they can but find people to buy all the shares,
   That your town will become the first place in the nation:
   You won't know the old town for the great alteration.

3 No drunken stage coachmen to break people's necks,
   Overturned into ditches, sprawled out on your backs;
   No blustering guard that through some mistake
   Fires his blunderbuss off if a mouse does but squeak.

4 Oh, no, my good friends, when the railroad is finished,
   All coachmen and cattle will for ever be banished;
   You ride up to London in two hours and a quarter,
   With nothing to drive you but a kettle of hot water.

5 You can breakfast at home on toast, tea and butter,
   And need not to put yourself all in a splutter;
   You may travel to London and dine there at noon
   And be home to your tea again the same afternoon.

6 What a beautiful sight it will be for to see
   A long string of carriages on the railway,
   All loaded with passengers inside and out,
   And moved by what comes from a tea kettle's spout.

7 As for packages, parcels and such kind of gear,
   There'll go more in one day than now goes in a year:
   'Twill be only to load about half a score waggons,
   Send a boiler along and then off they'll be jogging.

8 As for coach horses that eat more corn in a year
   Than'll maintain three parts of the labouring poor,
   They are all to be taken to the fellmonger's yard,
   And converted if possible to pork sausages and lard.

9 All great coach proprietors that have rolled in their wealth
   Are to ride upon donkeys for the good of their health,
   And to keep up their spirits are to strike up a theme
   Of the blessings of railroads and the virtue of steam.

10 As for innkeepers and ostlers and all such riff-raff,
   This railroad will drive them before it like chaff;
   They must 'list for her Majesty, the great Queen of Spain,
   But never come back to Old England again.

11 So these are a few of the strange alterations
   This wonderful railroad will make in the nation;
   If the shareholders be not careful and mind what they're after,
   They may all get blown up by this boiler of hot water.

Great Western Railroad: the authorising act of Parliament was passed in 1835 and the line from London to Bristol was opened in 1841. When 'tis finished . . . in two years: the ballad must therefore have appeared in 1839, or possibly a little earlier, since the line was opened later than anticipated. Cattle: coach horses (see page 11). Inside and out: see illustration on page 45. Waggons: see page 13. Fellmonger: seller of horse pelts and flesh. Queen of Spain: probably Maria Christina, widow of Ferdinand IV, who was regent of Spain for a time during the infancy of her daughter, the future Queen Isabella. Maria Christina had to face a rebellion by Carlists and a British legion fought on her side from 1835-7. This reference again helps to date the appearance of the song.

The singer of this rather lengthy street ballad would no doubt have made a selection of the verses which appealed to him. It has a variety of themes from which he could choose: praise for the railway and delight at its novelty, a malicious glee at the demise of the coaching industry and all concerned with it, and a certain scepticism about railway mania (the last verse giving a punning warning). There is little in the song of the epic struggle which resulted in the opening of the G.W.R., though there is a clear realisation of the changes likely to follow. A very similar ballad was published, probably in 1840, on another line, under the title of *The Wonderful Effects of the Leicester Rail Road* (see Roy Palmer, *A Touch on the Times*, 1974, p. 52).

Song 11 *Railroad travelling, or, A roide i' th' sixpenny go*

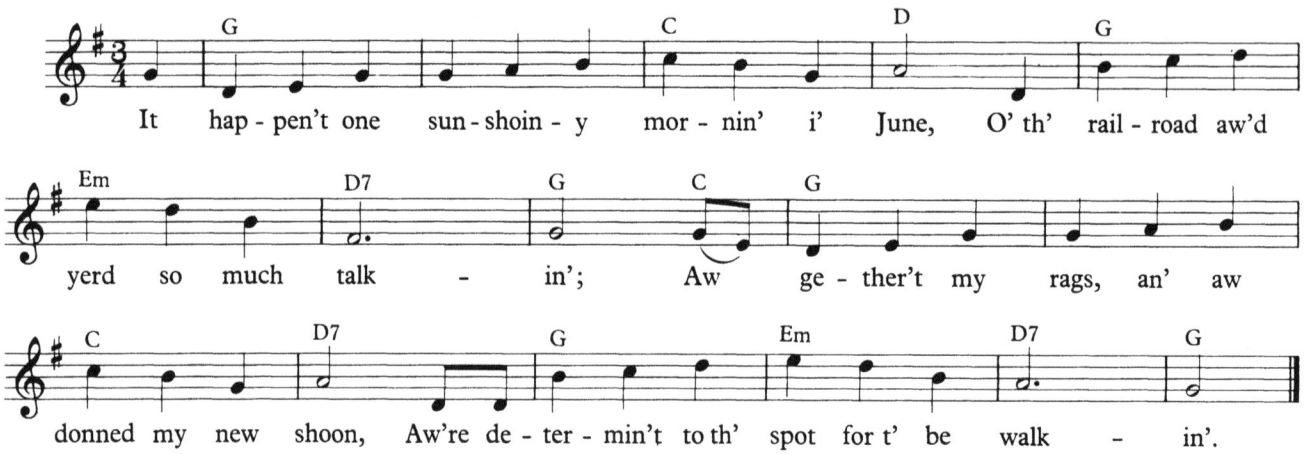

It hap-pen't one sun-shoin-y mor-nin' i' June, O' th' rail-road aw'd yerd so much talk - in'; Aw ge-ther't my rags, an' aw donned my new shoon, Aw're de-ter-min't to th' spot for t' be walk - in'.

2 Th' fost thing for a ticket to th' office aw crop:
   By th' mass bur ther's conjurin' in it;
   Th' mon hov up a lid, an' deawn it went – flop;
   He'd printed it o in a minet.

3 Then a mon wi' a chimney-sweep sign on his broo
   Show'd me th' road in a spot loike a pinfowt,
   For they'n rail't it aw reawnd, an' ther's gates for t' goo throo,
   An' a thing loike a stile for t' goo into it.

4 So aw thrutch't in among, an' look't reawnd for a form,
   But o' seats ther' wur noan to be fun;
   Then aw lippent full soon as ther'n too big a swarm
   O' boath ladies an' gentlemen gun.

5 An' o' trades besoide ther' wur cobblers and tayliers,
   Country Johnnies a ruck, an' some factory chaps, too;
   Just aside o' wheer aw stood wur so'diers an' sayliers,
   As ud got leaf for t' com' on a bit o' furloo.

6 Ther' wur Scotchmen an' Welshmen, an' bar-fute Paddy,
   A big fat butcher, noan wi' thick-toliola fed;
   An' some laafin' young wenches, donned up so pratty,
   Fit for t' mak' one repent ut they'd ever bin wed.

7 Th' owd skoomestur, too, wi' his lanky-lean son,
   For a bread-an'-cheese feight booath seem'd i' good fettle;
   An' a tinker stood theer, wi' his hommer an' pon –
   An' aw darsay he'd mended somebody's kettle.

8 Aw wur reet i' one corner, noather sittin' nor stondin',
   Bur, quietly loike, just takkin' th' stock,
   When my unlucky chops, beawt a moment o' warnin',
   Wur o at once sarve't wi' a thunderin' good knock.

9 Scoop, scoop, th' engine went, at a bonny owd speed,
   Throo th' air we soon fun eawrsels dartin';
   T'one bridge after t'other flew over my yed,
   Like a hawk when it follows a martin.

10 Aw wur moindin' my face, for aw felt it full sore,
   When ther' coom such a blaych o' cowd wind;
   Then aw gript fast to th' side, bur my hat it went o'er,
   An' wur laft monny a furlow behind.

11 'Stop, stop', aw cried out, 'Ther's a mon lost his hat',
   Whoile ther'n laughter i' every face;
   Nor a toothful a stop, still faster we shot,
   Loike owd Gilpin when runnin' a race.

12 Then i' Rushfort we stopt, an a rush ther' wur for t',
   For, loike leetnin', we rush't on again;
   Across Manchester alleys we'rn sent with a whiz,
   Neck an' crop – we could hardly tell when.

13 Wi' my yure stood straight up, loike a bundle o' sticks,
   Aw labbert my shammocks o'er th' boothers;
   For a hat reet slap up, aw pay'd deawn four-an'-six,
   An' surely it cover't my shoothers.

14 Bur aw're loike for t' com back, so aw ventur't my wride,
   Wonst moor, up'o' th' mersy o' steeum;
   Ther'n a gentlemon's pleck, so aw crop i' th' insoide
   For a shillin', wheer nobdy con see 'um.

15 Bur that's noan hauve so gradely, for nowt could aw feel,
   Till again Stopport pavors aw leet on;
   An' aw sed to mysel, aw may think very weel,
   At aw'm here wi' my yed an' my feet on.

16 Bur yo' tak my tip – if yo'n journey for t'goo,
   An' yo' hanno' mitch time t' get back;
   Ger i' th' sixpenny perch, an' it's o yo'n for t' do,
   An' yo'n find yoresel' theer in a crack.

17 Only, heaw yo' ger in, when it's time for t' begin –
   Moind; an' heaw yo ger eawt – when it stops.
   An' this sope o' advice aw shall awlus put in –
   Tak' care o' yo're hat, an' yo're chops.

Like much writing which attempts to convey dialect pronunciation, the words of this song are much more intelligible when spoken aloud than read silently. The dialect can be softened, if desired, by substituting standard words. Alternatively, the words can be rewritten, place names included, to suit a different locality and dialect. Schoon: shoes. Crop: crept. Conjurin': magic. He'd printed it o in a minet: he'd printed it all in a minute. This is a description of the printing of a ticket. The process was invented by Thomas Edmondson, a clerk on the Newcastle and Carlisle Railway, and introduced in 1839 on the Manchester and Leeds line. Chimney-sweep sign: presumably the company badge. Broo: brow, forehead. Pinfowt: pinfold – the platform. Thrutch't in: thrust in (to the carriage). Form: bench. O' seats ther' wur noan to be fun: of seats there were none to be found. Lippent: expected. Gun: going. A ruck: a lot. Furloo: furlough, leave. Bar-fute: bare-foot. Toliola: porridge. Pratty: pretty. Skoomestur: schoolmaster. Bread-an'-cheese feight: bread and cheese fight – a meal. Pon: pan. Beawt: without. Eawrsels: ourselves. Blaych: blast. Furlow: furlong. Nor a toothful a stop: not a mite did we stop. Gilpin: hero of a ballad by the poet, William Cowper, *The Journey of John Gilpin* (1783). Rushfort: Rusholme? Yure: hair. Labbert: lifted. Shammocks: feet. Boothers: boulders. Four-an'-six: four shillings and sixpence, the price of the hat. Shoothers: shoulders. Wonst moor: once more. Mersy: mercy. Gentlemon's pleck: gentleman's place – a first class carriage. Hauve: half. Stopport pavors: Stockport paving stones. Leet on: alight on. In a crack: in an instant.

Seats were not provided in the early days of railways in third-class compartments. Even as late as the middle 1840s, writes Hamilton Ellis, 'third-class passengers were treated as badly as the letter of the law would allow, the law being Gladstone's Act (of 1844), which gave them twelve miles an hour, protection from the weather, and one train daily at a penny a mile. At that time, first class was high-caste, second class was low-caste, and third class outcast.'

Railroad Travelling is an early, and vivid, reaction to railway travelling, having been written in the early 1840s by John Stoyls, a 'rhymester' from Denton, near Manchester. The ballad had this introduction:

'For my part, aw con mak' no sense o' Denton fowk; they noather known nowt, not mayna' weel, for they ne'er hossen goo nowheer for t' see it, bur stoppen cruddle't upo' ther' harston, awhoam. [For my part, I can make no sense of Denton people, they neither know anything, nor are they likely to do so, since they never dare to go anywhere to see it, but stay curled up on their hearthstones, at home.]

'Th'owd parson o' th' pleck aside o' Mottram used for t' say, "Nobbur for th' march o' hintellect, the'dden be nowt but a set of higniramuses". An aw've yerd say as th' railroads wur a sign o' th' march o' hintellect, bur aw conno' gawm heaw that con be so. What's the marchin' getten to do wi' th' railroad? – it's moor loike flyin' than marchin'; aye, an' yo'n say so, too, when yo'n read thro' th' whol' o' this papper, an' aw should loike o' th' principle inhabitants o' Denton for t' read it, an tak' care on it, an' let it goo fro' feyther to son – reet deawn to ther honsesters.'

One cannot speak for 'th' principle inhabitants o' Denton', but there is no question but that far more people travelled with the coming of railways. 'The Liverpool and Manchester from the start carried twice as many passengers as the old coaches had done, thus creating a new traffic. By 1851 the railways were carrying 80 million passengers a year (excluding season-ticket holders), by 1881 over 600 million, by 1901 over 1,100 million', wrote Harold Perkin.

The workmen's penny train arrives at Victoria station. The London-Chatham-Dover Railway launched an experimental scheme in about 1865, issuing cheap tickets to London workmen for a shilling a week

Autobiography of a Navvy

I was born at Wimbush, near Saffron Walden, in Essex. My father was a labouring man, earning nine shillings a week at the best of times; but often his wages were reduced to seven shillings. There was a wonderful large family of us – eleven was born, but we died down to six. I remember, one winter, we was very bad off, for we boys could get no employment, and no one in the family was working but father. He only got fourteen pence a day to keep eight of us in firing and everything. It was a hard matter to get enough to eat.

The first work ever I did was to mind two little lads for a farmer. I drawed them about in a little cart, for which I got my breakfast and a penny a day. When I got older I went to tending sheep. I was about seven year old then. I stopped in that place two years. [Later] after I left home, I started on the road 'tramping' about the country, looking for work. Sometimes I'd stop a few weeks with one master and then go on again, travelling about; never long at a time in the one place.

This is the way we used to carry on. Perhaps I'd light on an old mate somewhere about the country, and we'd go rambling together from one place to another. If we earned any money, we'd go to a public house, and stop there two or three days, till we'd spent it all, or till the publican turned us out drunk and helpless, to the world. Having no money to pay for a lodging, we had to lie under a hedge, and in the morning we'd get up thinking, 'What shall we do?' 'Where shall we go?' and perhaps it would come over us, 'Well, I'll never do the like again.'

We'd wander on till we could find a gang of men at work at some railroad or large building; sometimes they would help us, and sometimes they would not.

I came away, till I could get some work in Sussex, as a 'tipper'. I got four shillings a day, working Sundays and all. I bid there eleven weeks till I had saved nine pounds, then I left to come to London by the train. There I got along with bad company, and spent three or four of my pounds, and then turned towards Derby, where I spent the rest of my money, and had to lie again in a stable. From there I walked into Yorkshire.

Then I went to work at Bradford, where I stayed about six or eight weeks. Here an engine was to start upon a new line; and the contractor gave us a load of beer (about four barrels) for the opening. I was not satisfied with the way the man drawed this beer; and so, as soon as his back was turned and the crowd all round us, so he could not see, three of us got hold of a barrel and rolled it down the hill and over the hedge, knocked in the head of it, and drank out of our hats, which we dipped in the cask. Not content with all this, we must still go to a public house and have some more; and there I bid, till the landlord throwed me out in the road, where I laid till morning, while the rain poured down, and the water ran off both sides of me.

It was not long after this that I got sent to prison. I was working at Hastings, when we struck there. The ganger he came up and reckoned three or four on us, and then he upped with his fist and knocked me down; and as fast as I got up he hit me down again. Says I, 'Well done, old chap! you're going it gradely; but you've got a rum 'un to deal with this time,' I says; 'you ain't a-going to serve me as you have some of the drivers – leathering on 'em just when you like.'

Another makes answer, and says, 'Go it, Black un,' he says (they used to call me 'Black un' when I was young), 'Go it, Black un, I'll come in and help you'; and he comed up and caught hold of the ganger while I horse-whipped him, for I was a driver then; and another of them joined us. They come and ta'en us the next day, and had us locked up in Lewes Jail; two of us got two months, and the other one month. We was all very happy and comfortable there, though we were kept rather short of victuals. There they learnt me to spin mops, and it was there that I got hold of most of my scholarship. I learned to read from the turnkey – a very nice man. He come and stand by my cell door and help me to a word whenever I asked him, and a church parson used to preach to us every morning of the week – and very good it was! It did me a deal of good going to prison, that time – it learned me to be a scholar and a better man.

When a working man don't hear anything but swearing, and jeering, and laughing all the week round, for month after month, he can't hardly get it out of his head again rightly; but, if somebody will come on the works at dinner-time, and read, or talk to us, the men will mostly like it, and be glad to listen. It always does some good, if it is only the being spoken to, now and then, like as if we was the same flesh and blood with other people. We are wonderful tender-hearted, too. A 'navvy' will cry the easiest thing as is. If you'll only talk a little good to him, you can make a navvy burst out crying like a child in a few minutes, if you'll only take him the right way. (Anon, 'Autobiography of a Navvy' in *Macmillan's Magazine*, vol. 5, 1861-2.)

Song 12 *Navvy on the line*

I am a navvy bold, that's tramped the country round, sir, To get a job of work, where any can be found, sir. I left my native home, my friends and my relations, To ramble up and down and work in various stations. *Chorus* I'm a navvy, don't you see, I'm a navvy in my prime; I'm a nipper, I'm a tipper, and I'm working on the line.

2 I left my native home on the first day of September,
   That memorable day I still do remember.
   I bundled up my kit, Sunday smock and cap put on, sir,
   And wherever I do go, folks call me happy Jack, sir.

3 I got a job of work in the lovely town of Bury,
   And working on the line is a thing that makes me merry.
   I can use my pick and spade, likewise my old wheelbarrow;
   I can court the lasses, too, but don't intend to marry.

4 I worked a fortnight there, and then it come to pay-day,
   And when I got my wages, I thought I'd have a play-day.
   And then a little spree in High Street went quite handy,
   Then I sat me down in Jenkinson's, beside a Fanny Brandy.

5 I called for a pint of beer, and bid the old wench drink, sir,
   But whilst she was a-drinking, she too at me did wink, sir.
   Well, then we had some talk; in the back we had a rally;
   Then jumped o'er brush and steel and agreed we'd both live tally.

6 They called for liquors freely, the jug went quickly round:
   That being my wedding day I spent full many a crown, sir;
   And when my brass was done old Fanny went a-cadging,
   And to finish up my spree I went and sloped my lodgings.

7 Oh now I'm going to leave the lovely town of Bury;
  I'm sorry for to leave you, chaps, for I always found you merry.
  So call for liquors freely and drink away, my dandy.
  Here's a health to happy Jack, likewise to Fanny Brandy.

Nipper: helper, assistant. Bury: the original has a blank here where the singer could insert any town which seems appropriate, subject to the rhyme (though he could also alter the last word of the next line if necessary). High Street: also blank in the original. Fanny Brandy: presumably navvy slang for a woman. Jumped o'er brush and steel: navvy wedding ceremony. Live tally: live as man and wife. Sloped: decamped from.

Navvies at work. This photograph was taken in the 1890s, probably on the Stockton to Whitby railway line

Song 13 *The iron horse*

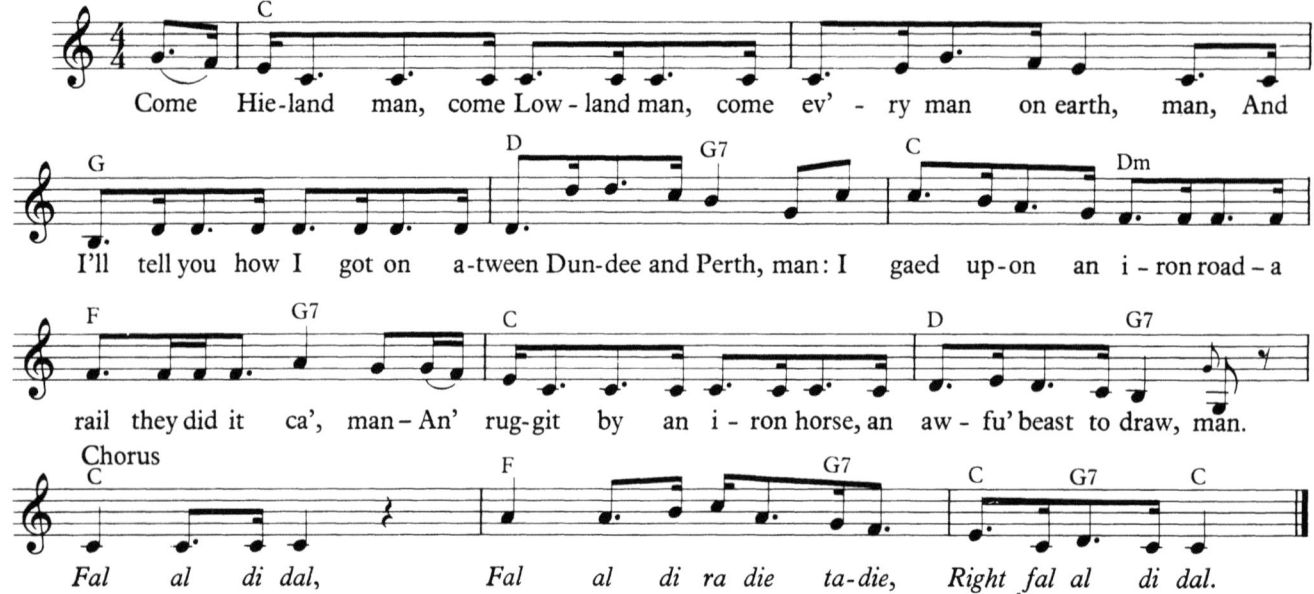

Come Hie-land man, come Low-land man, come ev'-ry man on earth, man, And I'll tell you how I got on a-tween Dun-dee and Perth, man: I gaed up-on an i-ron road-a rail they did it ca', man— An' rug-git by an i-ron horse, an aw-fu' beast to draw, man.

Chorus: Fal al di dal, Fal al di ra die ta-die, Right fal al di dal.

2 Then first and foremost, near the door, there was a wee bit wicket,
   It was there they gar'd me pay my ride, and they gied me a ticket;
   I gaed awa' up through the house, sat down upon a kist, man,
   To tak' a look o' a' I saw on the great big iron beast, man.

3 There was houses in a lang straught raw, a' stannin' upon wheels, man,
   And then the chiels that fed the horse were as black as a pair o' deils, man;
   And the ne'er a thing they gae the brute, but only coals to eat, man –
   He was the queerest beast that e'er I saw, for he had wheels for feet, man.

4 A chap cam' up, and round his cap he wore a yellow band, man,
   He bade me gang and tak' my seat. Says I, 'I'd rather stand, man.'
   He speer'd if I was gaun to Perth. Says I, 'And that I be, man,
   But I'm weel enough just whaur I am, because I want to see, man.'

5 He said I was the greatest fool that e'er he saw on earth, man,
   For t'was just the houses on the wheels that gaed frae this to Perth, man;
   And then he laughed and wondered hoo I hadna mair discernment,
   Says I, 'The ne'er a ken kent I: I thought the hale concern went.'

6 The beast it roared, and aff we gaed, through water, earth and stanes, man;
   We ran at sic an awfu' rate I thought we'd brak' oor banes, man.
   Till by and by we stoppit at a place ca'd something Gowrie,
   But ne'er a word had I to say, but only sit and glower aye.

7 Then after that we made a halt, and in comes Yellow Band, man:
   He asked me for the ticket and I a' my pouches fand, man;
   But ne'er a ticket I could get – I'd tint it on the road, man –
   So he gar'd me pay for't ower again, or else gang aff to quod, man.

8 Then after that we crossed the Tay and landit into Perth, man;
I vow it was the queerest place that e'er I saw on earth, man;
For the houses and the iron horse were far aboon the land, man,
And hoo they got them up the stairs I canna understand, man.

9 But noo I'm safely landit and my feet are on the sod, man
When I gang to Dundee again I'll tak' anither road, man;
Though I should tramp upon my feet till I'm not fit to stand, man,
Catch me again when I'm ta'en in wi' a chap in a yellow band, man.

Gaed: went. Ruggit: pulled. Wicket: small door. Gar'd: made. Kist: chest. Raw: row. Chiels: men. Deils: devils. Speer'd: asked. Mair: more. The ne'er a ken kent I: I had no knowledge of it. Hale: whole. Stanes: stones. Sic: such. Banes: bones. Ca'd: called. Something Gowrie: Blairgowrie (town in Perthshire). Glower aye: glower all the time. Pouches: pockets. Fand: felt in. Tint: lost. Quod: jail. Aboon: above.

This song, first sung in public at a festival of railway employees held at Perth in 1848, was written by Charles Balfour who was stationmaster at the time at Glencarse, between Dundee and Perth. Verses 4 and 5 were based on Balfour's experience when he was a guard: 'One day a sailor with his chest entered the Dundee station bound for Arbroath. He had never seen a railway before, and pitching his chest from his shoulder on to the platform he quietly sat down on top of it, as if to wait the course of events. 'Well, Jack,' said Mr B., 'are you for Arbroath?' 'Yes'. 'Well, then, you had better take your seat at once.' 'I think I'll do nicely here, mate.' 'But you must get into the train, you know.' 'Oh, hang the train,' ejaculated the sailor. 'I thought the whole concern went.' (Robert Ford, *Vagabond Songs and Ballads of Scotland*, Paisley and London, 1899-1901).

A train passing Wylam Scars on the Newcastle and Carlisle Railway. From J. W. Carmichael's Views on the Newcastle and Carlisle Railway, *published in 1836-8. Notice the passengers travelling on the outside of the first two carriages as was usual on stage coaches; the third-class passengers can be seen in the open waggons on the left*

Song 14 The Greenock railway

2   The ladies were all Pat's delight,
   And he sat down among their whites;
   I once was wrong but now I'm right,
   This morning on the railway.
   A gent sat there with curly hair;
   At Paddy he began to stare,
   And said he had not paid his fare
   For that class on the railway.

3   Then Paddy's blood began to rise;
   He took that spalpeen by surprise,
   And hit him straight between the eyes,
   That morning on the railway.
   The people all then made a fuss,
   To get the conductor in they must;
   But Pat told him to enter if he durst,
   That morning on the railway.

4   But now in sight of Glasgow town,
   And at the station we came down;
   They looked if a police could not be found
   To drag me from the railway.
   So now my shillelagh quick I drew,
   The conductor on the ground I threw,
   And then with legs so swift I flew,
   And left them at the railway.

5   Now to the harvest I will go
   And tell them there of all I know;
   I'll tell them of each friend and foe
   That I met on the railway.
   Then off to Ireland I'll repair
   And tell them all the wonders there,
   For never one in the county Clare
   Ever saw or heard of a railway.

Greenock: port on the River Clyde, 23 miles from Glasgow. Sixpence: 2½p. Whites: light-coloured clothes. That class: presumably the Irishman has got into a first class compartment by mistake. Spalpeen: rascal. Conductor: ticket inspector. Shillelagh: cudgel (pronounced 'shillayli'). To the harvest: the Irishman was a migrant worker who had travelled to Scotland to work in the harvest fields. The ballad is by no means lacking in sympathy for him.

Edinburgh, Glasgow, Greenock and Ayr were all linked by railway as early as 1842. The ballad probably dates from some time between then and the next ten or fifteen years.

A Twickenham railwayman

I was mad to become an engine driver. So, unbeknown to my people [in 1897, at the age of fourteen and a half], I went down and saw the foreman and in them days you had to give a sample of your writing and do three sums – multiplication, addition and subtraction, before they'd let you go and see the doctor. Well, within a week they sent for me and I hadn't then told my parents about it. I went to work, the first day, cleaning, with a white shirt on, hard hat and an attaché case. I've no need to tell you what I looked like when I came back!

You stopped at cleaning for three years – your money went up from 2/2d. to 2/4d. and then 2/6d. [see page 10]. Then they put you with the fitters and you had to put a twelvemonth in along with the fitter, as his mate, and they gave you 3/-d. a day. If there wasn't a vacancy with the fitters, they put you with the boiler makers and you worked with them for 3/-d. a day. Then you became what they called a turner's mate – a turner's the man that puts the engines in the shed at night when they come in, in the order they've got to go out in the morning. And that was all-night work and you still retained your 3/-d. a day. Then you became a fireman on the little six-foot coupled shunting engines and your money jumped up 3d. – 3/3d. a day. Eventually you got to firing on a passenger engine when your money became 3/6d. a day.

Well, after you'd done so many years on there you had to go to London and do five years at Nine Elms. There were several different gangs at Nine Elms. Anyhow, you worked your way up till you eventually became a main line fireman and your money was still 4/6d., but, for instance, I'd have to go from London to Exeter, perhaps with a heavy goods train, and I shuttled ten ton of coal during that trip and when I got there I'd earned a day and a half's pay, 6/3d., and I'd shifted ten ton of coal. That's besides getting my engine ready in the morning and cleaning her up when I got into the depot at night. It was all-night work. And it used to be the same to go to Weymouth or Dorset and the same when you went with the heavy milk trains to Yeovil.

Then to become a driver when your turn came, you had to pass a complete morning with an inspector. After you'd passed him, you were sent to Eastleigh to do the same examination on paper work. If you passed that you had to come back to London, see the company's doctor and pass him and pass an eye-sight test. If you passed all them, you became a driver and you started driving on 6/-d. a day. And you worked up till you got to a passenger driver, round here locally – any local drivers – at 7/6d. a day. On the main line I was given 8/6d. a day – that was the highest rate – but you was a *driver*. I'll tell you what I mean by that. I could come round from Waterloo to Waterloo with the densest fog there was – and we used to have fogs in them days – and I could tell you within a few yards where I was, anytime of the track, by the sound of the rail, by the sound of the bridges – you got so used to it. (Arthur Brazier, *West Twickenham in the 1890s: A Railwayman's Memories*, Borough of Twickenham Local History Society, 1976.)

Liverpool Station on 15 September 1830, the opening day of the Liverpool and Manchester Railway. The Duke of Wellington attended the celebrations. His special train is on the left in the picture

A COPY OF VERSES ON THE
33 RAILWAY PASSENGERS BURNT TO DEATH
In the Irish Mail Train, near
ABBERGELE, NORTH WALES, AUGUST 20TH, 1868.

H. Andrews, Printer, 26 & 27, St. Peter's Street, Leeds.

Oh listen with attention, good people far and near,
And when you hear this tale it will make you shed a tear;
Thirty-three people lost their lives, how sad it is to say,
While travelling on the Chester line, and Holyhead railway.

At the well-known town of Chester gay youth and
    beauty bright,
Had entered in those carriages upon that fatal night,
To cross the Irish Channel with the next mail did intend,
Not thinking for a moment they would meet with such an end

Some waggons loaded with oil that evening we find
They broke away with a frightful crash rolled down the incline,
And came in contract with the mail, the oil it did ignite,
And soon the train was in a flame—oh! it was a dreadful sight.

There was Lord and Lady Farnham, also servents and friends,
Who by this sad disaster met with an awful end,
The flames they spread like lightning, all help it was in vain,
Thirty-three were killed and burnt to death in that fatal train.

They left their friends lamenting at home in grief and sorrow,
There's no one can tell to day what may occur to-morrow;
There are none on earth what before this night we see
Like those that's in the grave, we in Death's cold arms may be

There are numbers now bewailing, and in sorrow to deplore,
For Death makes no distinction between the rich and poor;
When Death calls for either rich or poor nothing can them save
The servents, lord and lady, went to an early grave.

Consider, friends and Christians, consider ere to late
Consider, think and ponder, upon that dreadful fate
Of those unhappy victims while riding in a railway train,
Who were hurried to the silent tomb, for ever to remain.

Price One Penny.

4

The ocean highway

Henry Bell's steamer Comet

First British steam passage-boat
On the 15th of August 1812, there appeared in the *Greenock Advertiser*, an *annonce* signed Henry Bell, and dated from the Helensburgh Baths, making the public aware that thereafter a steam passage-boat, the *Comet* would ply on the Clyde between Glasgow and Greenock, leaving the former city on Tuesdays, Thursdays, and Saturdays, and the latter on the other lawful days of the week; the terms 4s. for the best cabin, and 3s. for the second. This vessel, one of only twenty-five tons burden, had been prepared in the building-yard of John and Charles Wood, Port-Glasgow, during the previous winter, at the instance of the above-mentioned Henry Bell, who was a simple uneducated man, of an inventive and speculative turn of mind, who amused himself with projects, while his more practical wife kept a hotel and suite of baths at a Clyde watering-place. The application of steam to navigation had been experimentally proved twenty-four years before, by Mr Patrick Miller, a Dumfriesshire gentleman, under the suggestions of Mr James Taylor, and with the engineering assistance of Mr Alexander Symington: more recently, a steamer had been put into regular use by Mr Robert Fulton, on the Hudson river in America. But this little *Comet* of Henry Bell, of the Helensburgh Baths, was the first example of a steam-boat brought into serviceable use within European waters. In its proposed trips of five-and-twenty miles, it is understood to have been successful as a commercial speculation; insomuch that, presently after, other and larger vessels of the same kind were built and set agoing on the Clyde. It is an interesting circumstance, that steam-navigation thus sprung up in a practical form, almost on the spot where James Watt, the illustrious improver of the steam-engine, was born. This eminent man appears never to have taken any active concern in the origination of steam-navigation; but, so early as 1816, when he, in old age, paid a visit to his native town of Greenock, he went in one of the new vessels to Rothesay and back, an excursion which then occupied the greater portion of a whole day. Mr Williamson, in his *Memorials of James Watt*, relates an anecdote of this trip. 'Mr Watt entered into conversation with the engineer of the boat, pointing out to him the method of *backing* the engine. With a footrule he demonstrated to him what was meant. Not succeeding, however, he at last, under the impulse of the ruling passion, threw off his overcoat and, putting his hand to the engine himself, shewed the practical application of his lecture. Previously to this, the *back-stroke* of the steamboat engine was either unknown, or not generally acted on. The practice was to stop the engine entirely, a considerable time before the vessel reached the point of mooring, in order to allow for the gradual and natural diminution of her speed.'

It is a great pity that Henry Bell's *Comet* was not preserved, which it would have been entitled to be, as a curiosity. It was wrecked one day [in December 1820], by running ashore on the Highland coast, when Bell himself was on board – no lives, however, being lost. The annexed representation of the proto-steamer of Europe, was obtained by Mr Williamson, from an original drawing which had been in the possession of Henry Bell, and was marked with his signature. (R. Chambers, *Book of Days*, 1862-3.)

Song 15 *The adventures of a steam packet*

*See the note with Song 10.
Verses 2-6 begin at double bar *a*, with the section from this to double bar *b* repeated to accommodate lines 3 and 4.
The song concludes at † after the singing of the final chorus.

2 In a boat I got afloat as clumsy as an elephant,
So spruce and gay to spend the day and make a splash.
Gad! it's true, I did it too; for, stepping in, I fell off on't,
And overboard, upon my word, I went slap dash.
Wife a-squalling, daughter bawling, everything provoking me;
Called a hog, a poodle dog, and all the sailors joking me.
So, dripping wet, and in a pet, with many more distressibles:
The fellow took the longboat hook and caught my inexpressibles.

3   Such a gig, without a wig, on deck I was exhibited,
    Ears a-whizzing, laughers quizzing, passengers and crew;
    I raved and swore than on the shore I rather had been gibbeted
    Than thus half-drowned by all around be roasted too.
    Danger past and dry at last, indulging curiosity,
    I stared to see the vessel flee with such strange velocity.
    'Oh, pray,' said I, to one hard by, 'what power can impel us so?'
    'The smoky devil goes by steam; at least the sailors tell us so.'

4   Not a sail to catch a gale, yet magically on we went,
    'Gainst wind and tide and all beside in wonder quite.
    Cast my eye up to the sky and, tall as London Monument,
    I saw the kitchen chimney smoke as black as night.
    People toiling, roasting, boiling, bless us such a rookery,
    They'd soup and fish, both fowl and flesh, a London tavern cookery.
    And then the noise of men and boys, a din, no, more, a fine hubbub,
    I thought the crew were devils too, the master called Beelzebub.

5   Wife drew near and said, 'My dear, oh now's your time to pick a bit;
    The dinner's served, so pray observe, how we must fly.'
    Says I, 'My dear, I'm very queer, I'm going to be sick a bit,
    I'm seized with an all-overness, I faint, I die.
    I cannot eat, I loath my meat, I feel my stomach failing me;
    Steward hasten, get a basin, what the deuce is ailing me?
    Now if it's handy, bring some brandy'. The malady to quench unable,
    Down I lay for half a day in pickle quite unmentionable.

6   As to dinner, I'm a sinner if I touched a bit of it;
    But anchor cast and home at last, we're safe, I see.
    In the packet, such a racket, crowding to get rid of it,
    And little wonder, blood and thunder, I'm on the quay.
    'How d'ye do?' and 'How are you?' 'I see you're better physically.'
    'Zounds, be still, I'm very ill, you're ever talking quizzically.'
    There's some with glee may go to sea but I shall not be willing, sirs,
    For such a day again to pay just two pounds fifteen shillings, sirs.

Lauk: Lord (exclamation). Inexpressibles: trousers. Gig: oddity. Monument: to the Great Fire of London. Rookery: densely populated place. Beelzebub: the devil.
   The song was sung in 1830 at the English Opera House in London by Mr Chapman. It was also printed as a street ballad which, most unusually, included both words and tune.

'In the eighteenth century a place like Margate was not difficult to reach by coach or diligence, changing at Canterbury, though most of the visitors came by boat. The famous Margate 'hoys', though primarily cargo-boats – they were one-masted corn-sloops – also carried some passengers, and by 1800 they landed as many as 18,000 passengers a year. Within twenty years they were succeeded by the steam-packets. The early steamboat was a sailing-vessel converted by the addition of paddle-wheels, a steam-engine to rotate them, and a chimney almost as tall as the masts to carry away the smoke. [See verse 4.]

'The "short-ferry" service went up the river to Kew and Richmond, and down to Woolwich and Greenwich, sharing the daily city traffic with the omnibuses; the "long ferry" service went down as far as Gravesend, and, by the thirties, was extended in the summer to Sheerness, Herne Bay, Margate, and Ramsgate. The development of the pleasure-steamer began the era of cheap holiday travel for the masses. It was not until after 1848 that the steamboats had to face the competition of the railways, which publicised not only cheap day-trips, but also the new idea of an annual middle-class holiday by the sea.

'At first the novel experience of a trip on a steamboat had elements of adventure.' (Christopher Pulling, *They Were Singing, and What They Sang About*, 1952, p. 57.)

Song 16 *The launch of the 'Great Britain'*

2 Now down the Hotwells they do flock,
   Rich, poor and old and young,
   To have a sight with all their might
   Fit to break their necks they'll run.
   To see her launched this glorious day,
   There's Bet so brisk and cosy,
   And peg-leg Poll from Lewin's Mead
   Will dance with Jim along Josey.

3 And then Prince Albert he is here
   To see her launched on water;
   And he has left behind at home
   His royal son and daughters.
   He'll treat the sailors (oh, what fun)
   To rum, gin, ale so frisky;
   He'll crack the bottles merrily
   And they'll swiggle down the whisky.

4 Oh, when that they have launched her off
   The stocks into the water,
   They'll tow her down with sailors bold
   And shouts from every quarter.
   They'll dance and sing and fiddle away,
   Like devils prance and hustle;
   A lady vowed she would be there
   If she pawned her boa and bustle.

5 There's red-nosed Kit from Temple Street
   And Nance with Mr Larket,
   And bandy-leg Sue from West Street came
   A-toddling down Old Market.
   She swears she'll have a good blow-out
   Of cabbage, greens and bacon,
   Besides some taters and cauliflowers
   And peas, if I'm not mistaken.

6 There's tailors, snobs and soldiers there,
  With their muskets they'll have capers;
  There's flitters, too, with hot pea-soup;
  Mr Fubbs with hot potatoes.
  They'll have, oh, dear, oh, such a lark
  When the launch it is quite over;
  They'll drink success to the *Great Britain*,
  To the Queen, her son and daughters.

Last chorus
Oh, the largest steamship in the world, Great Britain *it is she,*
And she is launched July nineteen, eighteen hundred and forty-three.

Hotwells: street in Bristol. Jim along Josey: fictional hero in a popular song of the same name. Tow her down: from the docks down the river Avon to the sea. Boa: fur or feather wrap. Bustle: skirt exaggeratedly padded behind. Snobs: cobblers. Flitters: fritters.

'Prince Albert caught a six o'clock train from Paddington to Bristol on the morning of 19 July 1843 to launch the steamship *Great Britain*. His Prince Consort status was appropriate to christening the world's largest and most revolutionary ship. As a man with a technical bent he would appreciate the purpose and ingenuity of innovations like fold-down masts, the vessel's double bottom, and watertight bulkheads. The all-iron fabric and screw propeller were the major and most advertised novelties in a ship of 2,984 tons displacement – up to then they had been used together only experimentally in large vessels and to a limited commercial extent in ships seven times smaller than the *Great Britain*. In addition the new ship had a balanced rudder – the very beginnings of power-assisted steering at sea – and an electric speed and distance log; both these refinements were ahead of their time. The 19 July 1843 was the day marine engineering made the great leap forward into modern times' (John O' Callaghan, *The Saga of the S.S. 'Great Britain'*, 1971, p. 13).

Few technical considerations come into our ballad, which, most unusually, prints the author's name, Thomas Cook, at the end. It is almost exclusively concerned with the vigorous celebrations which accompanied the launch. At least two other 'new songs on the launch' appeared at the same time.

19 July 1843 was a festive occasion. Thousands of people flocked to Bristol to watch the launching of Brunel's great ship

Song 17 *The wreck of the 'Royal Charter'*

2 From far Australia with a pleasant gale
   The *Royal Charter* for old England had sailed
   With her human cargo, but the fates did rule
   She never more would reach Liverpool.

3 For nine long hours this vessel brave
   Was tempest-tossed on the stormy wave;
   But in Moelfre Bay, without mast or sails,
   She was drove in pieces on the coast of Wales.

4 On Wednesday morning I grieve to say
   Her fore and mainmast were cut away;
   Our mizzentop fell with a heavy crash,
   As the raging waves o'er the ship did dash.

5 Now Captain Taylor with his seamen brave
   Used all their efforts the ship to save;
   But notwithstanding all they could do
   The *Royal Charter* she broke in two.

6 Now broadside on she drove on shore,
   The lightning flashed and the sea did roar;
   Brave Captain Taylor was drowned, it's true,
   With ninety-seven of his gallant crew.

7 The total number that lost their lives
   Was four hundred and fifty-five;
   Of women and children we are assured,
   Not one escaped out of all on board.

8 O God, 'tis frightful to think what crowds
   Of drowning passengers clung to the shrouds;
   To hear their shrieks on the stormy sea
   As from the vessel they were washed away.

9 May the Lord look down on the deep distress
   Of the widowed mother and the fatherless,
   Likewise the parents of the seamen brave
   Who in the *Royal Charter* met a watery grave.

*The last line of each verse may be repeated.

Beaumaris: in Anglesey. In fact the wreck was several miles from Beaumaris, on the north-east coast of the island at Moelfre Bay, pronounced 'Moilvrey' (see verse 3).

The *Royal Charter*, launched on the River Dee in 1855, was an iron sailing ship of over 2500 tons with an auxiliary steam engine. On her maiden voyage to Australia she made a record passage of 59 days between Plymouth and Melbourne. She was wrecked in October, 1859, when homeward bound for Liverpool with 493 passengers and crew and a cargo which included £4,000,000 worth of gold.

She arrived off Point Lynas, the extreme north-eastern tip of Anglesey, at 9 p.m. on Tuesday 25 October, just as a violent storm blew up from the north-east. Both anchors were dropped, but the cables parted. The engine was not powerful enough to prevent the ship from drifting on to the jagged rocks of Moelfre Bay. For some nine hours the ship was battered on the rocks, until it broke up. A seaman called Joseph Rogers managed to get a rope ashore. By this means 39 people were saved. All the rest perished. There is a monument in Llanallgo Churchyard to 140 of the victims who were buried there.

LIVERPOOL & AUSTRALIAN NAVIGATION COMPANY.
Steam from Liverpool to Australia,
UNDER 60 DAYS.

The ROYAL CHARTER'S extraordinary passage of 59 days to Melbourne is the fastest ever made.

THE MAGNIFICENT STEAM CLIPPER
"ROYAL CHARTER,"
2719 Tons Register and 200 Horse Power, with Fire-proof and Water-tight Compartments,

F. BOYCE, COMMANDER,

IS APPOINTED TO LEAVE THE RIVER MERSEY FOR

MELBOURNE, PORT PHILIP,
ON THURSDAY, 2nd OCTOBER.

This noble Steam Clipper, built expressly for the Company, one of the finest models yet constructed, combines all the advantages of a Steamer with those of a Clipper Sailing Ship, and offers the only opportunity yet presented to the Public of certainty in the time required for the voyage. She has just made the extraordinary passage of **59 days to Melbourne**—a performance never before accomplished. On this voyage she ran one day 358 knots, during which she attained the astonishing speed of 18 nautical miles in the hour. Her daily average for the whole distance to Melbourne was 222¾ knots, or 10½ miles per hour. Her accommodations for all classes of Passengers are unrivalled.

FARES TO MELBOURNE.
AFTER SALOON...60, 65, and 75 Guineas. | SECOND CLASS,......25 and 30 Guineas.
THIRD CLASS.................16, 18, and 20 Guineas.

Including Stewards' Fees, the attendance of an experienced Surgeon, and all Provisions of the best quality, except Wines, Spirits, and Malt Liquors, which will be supplied at very moderate prices on board.

Children from One to Twelve Years, Half Price. Infants free.

Passengers booked to be forwarded by the First Opportunity after arrival to SYDNEY, ADELAIDE, HOBART-TOWN, &c., at an extra charge of 7 and 8 Guineas 1st Class; 4 and 5 Guineas 2nd Class; 3 and 4 Guineas 3rd Class.

In the AFTER SALOON every requisite will be provided, including Beds, Berths, Bedding, Plate, Table Linen, Crockery, Glass, &c.; supplied with the best articles of Food, and an abundant Dietary Scale. Live Stock, Poultry, &c.

The AFTER SALOON is fitted with Ladies' Boudoir, Baths, &c., &c., &c.

DECK.—The Poop aft is appropriated to the After Saloon Passengers alone. The Deck amidships to the First and Second Class Passengers, and forward to the Third Class Passengers.

No Passenger can be accommodated in a State-room by himself, so long as he can be placed with other passengers, unless the State-room is specially arranged for; Berths may be changed, if necessary, unless a whole State-room is secured.

DEPOSITS.

One-half of the passage-money must be paid before a Berth can be secured. The Berths are appropriated in rotation as the Deposits are paid. Passengers in the country can have Berths secured by enclosing a Bank or Post-office order to the undersigned for half the amount of passage, and they are requested to give their Christian names, ages, and trades, and if married, names and ages of each member of the family.

LUGGAGE.
THE REGULATIONS BELOW WILL BE STRICTLY ADHERED TO.

Forty Cubic Feet allowed each Adult Passenger in After Saloon
Thirty do.   "   "   Second Class
Twenty do.   "   "   Third do.
Children in proportion.

Freight on any excess, not exceeding 10 feet, will be charged at 3s. per foot. If, however, the excess be more than 10 cubic feet, it must be previously engaged as cargo. Such overplus must be along side the vessel six days prior to sailing, *or it cannot be taken on board*; and unless specially engaged previously, cannot be taken if the ship is full.

PASSENGERS MUST TAKE CHARGE OF THEIR LUGGAGE UNTIL ON BOARD SHIP.

Before Luggage can go on board all Passage-money to be paid. The Luggage to be distinctly marked with Paint, two inches long, with the owners name and destination, (*and cannot be delivered elsewhere,*) State-rooms, Berths, and Cabins to which it belongs.

The owner's are not responsible for loss or damage to Luggage. Merchandise cannot be carried as Luggage. All Bullion, Specie, Watches, Jewellery, or Treasure, above the value of £150, must be declared, and pay the Freight.

DOGS are charged £5 each.

SERVANTS.—Females are charged one-half After Saloon Fare. Men Servants are charged Third Class Fare, and are berthed and provided accordingly.

All Extra Luggage must be alongside by Saturday the 27th September. All other Luggage (Hat Boxes and Carpet Bags excepted) on Monday the 29th Sep. She will proceed into the river on Tuesday, the 30th. A Steamer will leave the Prince's Pier-head at 9 o'clock on the morning of the 1st October, when all except Saloon Passengers must be on board. Saloon Passengers embark on Thursday, the 2nd

The Shipwreck of the Royal Charter

Never had I seen a year going out, or going on, under quieter circumstances. Eighteen hundred and fifty-nine had but another day to live and truly its end was Peace on that seashore that morning . . .

Yet, only two short months had gone, since a man, living on the nearest hill-top overlooking the sea, being blown out of bed at about daybreak by the wind that had begun to strip his roof off, and getting upon a ladder with his nearest neighbour to construct some temporary device for keeping his house over his head, saw from the ladder's elevation as he looked down by chance towards the shore, some dark troubled object close in with the land. And he and the other descending to the beach, and finding the sea mercilessly beating over a great broken ship, had clambered up the stony ways, like staircases without stairs, on which the wild village hangs in little clusters, as fruit hangs on boughs, and had given the alarm. And so, over the hill-slopes, and past the waterfall, and down the gullies where the land drains off into the ocean, the scattered quarrymen and fishermen inhabiting that part of Wales had come running to the dismal sight – their clergyman among them. And as they stood in the leaden morning, stricken with pity, leaning hard against the wind, their breath and vision often failing as the sleet and spray rushed at them from the ever forming and dissolving mountains of sea, and as the wool which was a part of the vessels cargo blew in with the salt foam and remained upon the land when the foam melted, they saw the ship's life-boat put off from one of the heaps of wreck; and first, there were three men in her, and in a moment she capsized, and there were but two; and again she was struck by a vast mass of water, and there was but one; and again, she was thrown bottom upward, and that one, with his arm struck through the broken planks and waving as if for the help that could never reach him, went down into the deep.

It was the clergyman himself from whom I heard this, while I stood on the shore, looking in his kind wholesome face as it turned to the spot where the boat had been. The divers were down then, and busy. They were 'lifting' today the gold found yesterday – some five-and-twenty-thousand pounds. Of three hundred and fifty thousand pounds' worth of gold, three hundred thousand pounds' worth, in round numbers, was at that time recovered. The great bulk of the remainder was surely and steadily coming up. Some loss of sovereigns there would be, of course; indeed, at first sovereigns had drifted in with the sand, and been scattered far and wide over the beach, like sea-shells; but most other golden treasure would be found. As it was brought up, it went aboard the Tug-steamer, where good account was taken of it. So tremendous had the force of the sea been when it broke the ship, that it had beaten one great ingot of gold, deep into a strong and heavy piece of her solid ironwork: in which, also, several loose sovereigns that the ingot had swept in before it, had been found, as firmly embedded as though the iron had been liquid when they were forced

The monument in Llanallgo churchyard, Anglesey, commemorating those who died in the wreck of the Royal Charter

there. It had been remarked of such bodies come ashore, too, as had been seen by scientific men, that they had been stunned to death, and not suffocated. Observation, both of the internal change that had been wrought in them, and of their external expression, showed death to have been thus merciful and easy. The report was brought, while I was holding such discourse on the beach, that no more bodies had come ashore since last night. It began to be very doubtful whether many more would be thrown up, until the north-east winds of the early spring set in. Moreover, a great number of the passengers, and particularly the second-class women-passengers, were known to have been in the middle of the ship when she parted, and thus the collapsing wreck would have fallen upon them after yawning open, and would keep them down. A diver made known, even then, that he had come upon the body of a man, and had sought to release it from a great super-incumbent weight; but that, finding he could not do so without mutilating the remains, he had left it where it was. (Charles Dickens, in *All the Year Round*, 28 January 1860.)

Hells afloat

On New Year's Day 1860 I left a good home and kind employer to wander I know not where. The only explanation I can give for such strange behaviour is that I had a great desire to travel; but not having the means to do so, the only way open to me was to go to sea and learn the duties of a sailor. At this time I was employed by a baker in London, and I had been so engaged for some months . . .

On arriving at the shipping office I was so very fortunate as to get a ship at once, for I had no sooner entered than the master of a vessel accosted me and said he wanted a boy. An agreement was at once entered into, and I was to go on board the same evening. The brig – for that was the rig of the vessel I had engaged to sail in – was in the Thames off

Deptford. I soon found my way on board the *Isabella* – my first ship – and of course everything was quite strange to me there. The next day sail was made, our destination being Shields. This was only a coasting trip, which deep-water sailors would laugh at if called 'going to sea'. Nevertheless, it was quite sea enough for me, just then at least, for we had rather a rough passage; but the thought never entered my head to abandon my idea of travelling.

Sea-sickness is far from being pleasant under any circumstances, and even those that have every comfort and can stay in bed dread that horrible sensation; but how about the poor boy who is compelled to go to the masthead? Many unkind people will say, 'Serve him right! He should have stayed at home.' But I think that even those people, if they had the slightest idea what a poor boy goes through at the masthead – or, more practically speaking, on the yard – cold, wet and sick, the motion of the ship being many more times rapid aloft than on deck, and knowing that the sail must be furled before he comes down, I think they would pity him, or they would be very hard-hearted indeed . . .

My eighteenth ship [in 1867] was the *Arkwright*, of New York, and was full-rigged. The *Arkwright* was one of those American packet ships sailing between New York and Liverpool, but now [1893] almost entirely superseded by steamers. I cannot find words wherewith to describe some of those ships in those days, unless by quoting a nautical phrase and say that they were 'hells afloat'. No one but those who have actually sailed in such ships can conceive the hardships endured by men crossing and recrossing that greatest highway of the ocean. These sailors – officers and men – were the hardest 'cases' that ever it was my lot to meet. As sailors they were the best the world could produce, for I have never seen men pick up a stiff-frozen sail in bad weather more quickly than they. What a contrast between those sailors and the 'cuckoo' sailors sailing in the steamers of the present day!

I was nineteen days crossing the Western Ocean in the *Arkwright*, and I should have been perfectly satisfied if the number had been less; for to give an illustration of some of the hardships endured I may state that I came on deck one morning at eight o'clock when on the Banks of Newfoundland, and was sent aloft to repair some rigging. When I came down at half-past twelve I scarcely knew whether there was life in me or not; had I been engaged in taking in sail I could have course have kept my blood circulating, but to continue aloft and in one position in midwinter amongst the fog on the Banks for four and a half hours was enough to freeze the upper hank of a Greenlander's jib. Many people will ask why I did not come down. I can only say to those that would ask this question that it was clear that they had never been 'packet rats' or they would know the reason why. (George Sorrell, *Man Before the Mast*, 1928.)

The wreck of the Royal Charter *off the coast of Anglesey in 1859*

Song 18 *The unseaworthy ship*

The doomed ship weighs an-chor, out she is bound, With car-go too heavy and timbers unsound; A storm overtakes her, reef, reef, ev'ry sail, But all to no purpose, she's lost in the gale. See the old vessel, now tossed on the waves, Telling her crew to prepare for their graves; Sent out insured, with a hope she'd go down, Not caring for widows and orphans at home.

Chorus
Honour to Plimsoll, his labour will save Thousands of brave men from watery graves. May his movement all our support adorn; His work will save thousands of lives yet unborn.

2 Out on the wild waves sailors must go,
  Earning bread for their children – what perils they know.
  In old, rotten craft, which ship agents procure,
  Brave men they are lost, in those vessels insured.
  The captain is anxious the vessel to save
  From the tempest which threatens a watery grave,
  But all human efforts can't keep her afloat;
  Oh, God! she is sinking, out, out with the boat.

3 Down with the life-boat, out on the waves,
  Hoping to find land or sight some vessel's sail;
  They pray to be saved but what can they do,
  Surrounded by wild waves, that boat and her crew?
  The storm it is raging, the billows they roll;
  No help it is near for to save those poor souls.
  The boat is upset, that brave crew is lost:
  This, this is the price which our rotten ships cost.

4 Out, out, ye landsmen, out with a will,
  Stand up in justice for Plimsoll's great Bill;
  Don't be rejected, it's on God's mission sent,
  But up, all as one man, before Parliament.
  The nation demands it, 'tis the widows' cry;
  The sailors' poor orphans we can't pass them by.
  Let us work, every soul, to help brave Plimsoll through,
  And then we may boast of our ships and their crews.

It is not clear which of Plimsoll's bills the songwriter has in mind, but the Unseaworthy Ships Bill of 1875 seems the most likely. The ballad is one of many in praise of Plimsoll, with titles like *Admirable Plimsoll* and *God Bless Plimsoll, the Sailors' Friend*.

Samuel Plimsoll's name is a household word because of the sports shoes called after him. However, the Plimsoll Line painted on ships to indicate safe levels of loading is his more important memorial.

He lived from 1824 to 1898. As member of Parliament for Derby from 1868 to 1880, he was an ardent social reformer. The most famous of his campaigns was for safety at sea and his main target was the 'coffin ships', overloaded and unseaworthy vessels which were heavily insured so that when they were lost, as frequently happened, the shipowners made a considerable profit.

Plimsoll attempted to introduce a parliamentary bill in 1871, but failed. He then wrote and published his famous appeal to the nation, *Our Seamen* (1873). Despite strong opposition from the shipowning interest, this helped to lead to the setting up of a Royal Commission 'To make Inquiry with regard to the alleged Unseaworthiness of British Registered Ships, whether arising from Overloading, Deckloading, Defective Construction, Condition, Form, Equipment or Machinery, Age or Improper Stowage; also to inquire into the present state of the Law as to the liability of ship owners for injury to those whom they employ, and the alleged practice of "Under-manning" ships, and to suggest amendments to the Law which might remedy or less such evils as may be found to have arisen from the matters aforesaid.'

The Commission's report was ineffectual. The load line for which Plimsoll had campaigned was not recommended. In 1875 he again put forward his own bill; instead the government (led by Disraeli who was hostile to Plimsoll) proposed an inadequate substitute. Plimsoll's fury led to a great scene in the House of Commons when he called other members villains. At last the government had to defer to the great wave of public support which arose for Plimsoll. His temporary Unseaworthy Ships Act became law in August 1875, and his Merchant Shipping Act of the following year permanently embodied the Plimsoll Line into English Law.

Song 19 *Strike the bell*

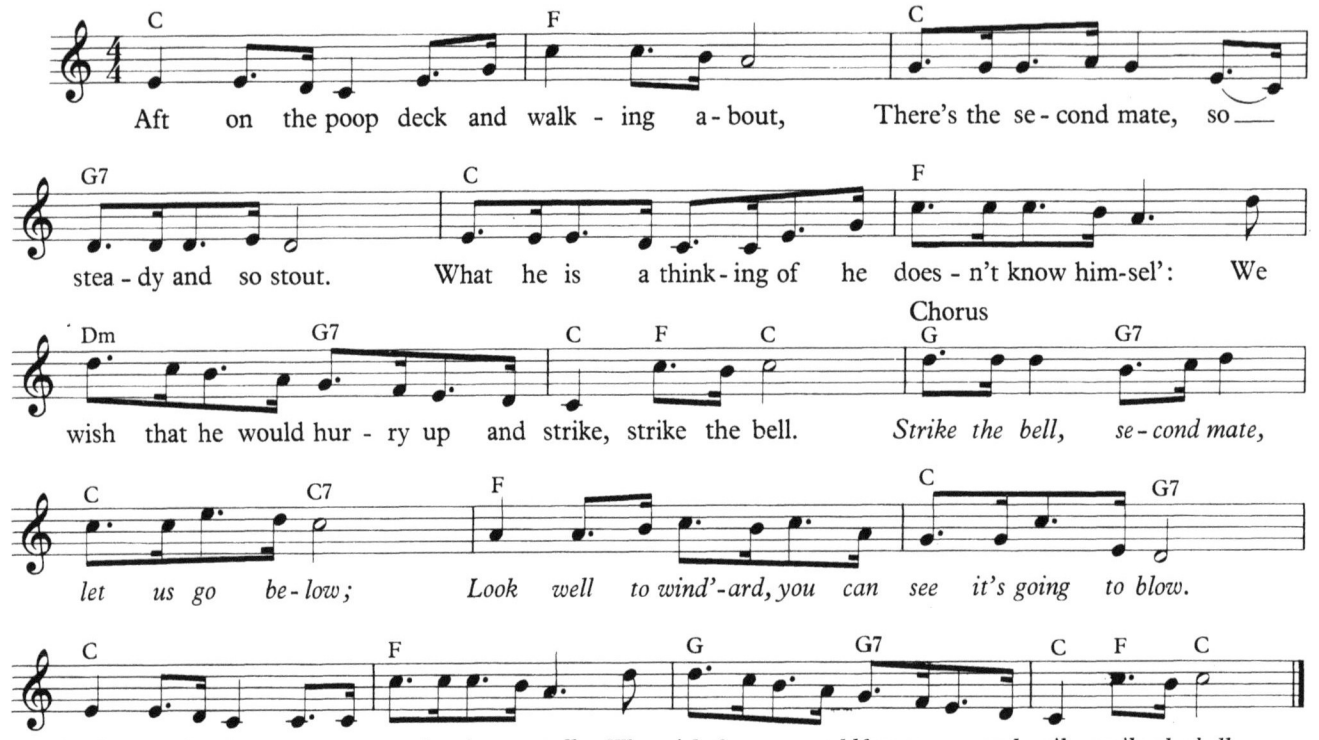

2 Down on the main deck and working at the pumps,
   There's the starboard watch all a-longing for their bunks;
   Looking out to wind'ard they see a great swell:
   They're wishing that the second mate would strike, strike the bell.

3 Aft at the wheel poor Anderson stands,
   Grasping at the wheel with his cold, mittened hands;
   Looking at the compass, oh, the course is clear as hell:
   He's wishing that the second mate would strike, strike the bell.

4 For'ard on the fo'c's'le head a-keeping sharp lookout,
   Young Johnny's standing, ready for to shout:
   'Lights are burning bright, sir, and everything is well.'
   He's wishing that the second mate would strike, strike the bell.

5 Aft on the quarterdeck the gallant captain stands,
   Looking out to wind'ard with a spy-glass in his hands;
   What he is a-thinking of we know very well:
   He's thinking more of shortening sail than striking the bell.

Aft: towards the stern. Poop: aftermost deck. Strike the bell: the passage of time on shipboard is divided into 'watches' (four-hourly periods) indicated by the ringing of a bell. So, noon, for example, the start of a watch, is one bell, 12.30 p.m., two bells, and so on until 4 p.m., eight bells. A new watch then begins and the same pattern of bells is repeated. Wind'ard: windward; direction from which the wind is blowing. Glass: barometer. Starboard watch all a-longing for their bunks: at 8 p.m. these men will be dismissed and have four hours to sleep before returning to duty at midnight. If the weather is bad they may have to remain on deck and assist with the working of the ship. For'ard on the fo'c's'le head: the foremost part of the ship. Lights are burning: 'Apprentices have to clean all the lamps aboard, and trim them every day: the sidelights (when used) being a particularly dirty job. It is common when a young apprentice in brass buttons sallies through "sailor towns" for scornful "shellbacks" to sing out at him, "Light the binnacle!" because of his always being called on at sea to trim that most necessary of all lights at night' (F. W. H. Symondson, *Two Years Abaft the Mast, or, Life as a Sea Apprentice*, 1876, p. 72). Quarterdeck: part of upper deck aft of mainmast; a place where captain traditionally stood when commanding the ship. Shortening sail: reducing sail area, either by reefing or taking in sails (or both).

This sailors' song, popular in the latter part of the nineteenth century, is based on *Ring the Bell, Watchman*, which the American songwriter, Henry Clay Work, wrote in 1865 to salute the end of the Civil War. The same tune made its way to Australia and was used for a shearing song, *Click go the shears*.

By the 1880s and 1890s sail had overwhelmingly lost the battle with steam, though some coastal vessels continued under sail well into the twentieth century. Indeed, so did a few deep-sea ships, as witness Eric Newby's fine account of his 1938 voyage in a four-masted barque (*The Last Grain Race*, 1972). Not only has sail, through the feats of men like Sir Francis Chichester, continued to capture our imaginations, but it seems that there is a possibility of wind-powered cargo ships in the future.

Manning the helm on a nineteenth-century sailing boat

Suggestions for further activities

Records

1. The following include songs (not necessarily in the same version) in this book:
No. 5. Under the title of *The Jolly Waggoner: The Watersons* (12T142, Topic Records Ltd, 27 Nassington Road, London NW3 2TX), and *Johnny's Private Army* (TSR020, Traditional Sound Recordings, 183 Chester Road, Macclesfield, Cheshire)
No. 8 TSR019/CS and *Garners Gay* (LP1006, English Folk Dance and Song Society, 2 Regent's Park Road, London NW1 7AY)
No. 12 *Steam Ballads* (BRO121, Broadside Records, Tettenhall, Wolverhampton)
No. 13 BRO121 and *Steam Whistle Ballads* (Topic 12T104)
No. 17 *Champions of Folly* (Topic 12TS256)
No. 19 *The Bitter and the Sweet* (Topic 12TS217)

2. Other useful collections of sea songs and shanties:
Farewell Nancy (Topic 12T110)
Sea Shanties (Topic 12TS234)
Sailormen and Servingmaids (Topic 12T194)
The Valiant Sailor (Topic 12TS232)
Across the Western Ocean (St-4, Swallowtail Records, 304 College Avenue, Ithaca, N.Y. 14850)
Whaling and Sailing Songs (TLP1005, Traditional Recordings, 10920 Wiltshire Blvd, Suite 410, Los Angeles, California 90024)
A Sailor's Garland (XTRA 5013, Transatlantic Records Ltd, 86 Marylebone High Street, London W1M 4AY)
As we were a-sailing (ZDA137, Argo Record Company Ltd, 115 Fulham Road, London SW3 6RR)
Ye Mariners All (Argo, ZDA138)
There is a good sound-picture of canal life, based largely on the BBC Sound Archives, on *Narrow Boat* (Argo, ZT142). See also *The English Canals* (BRO118) and *The Bold Navigators* (TSR019).

Books

General
V. T. J. Arkell, *Britain Transformed*, Penguin, 1973
Hugh Bodey, *Discovering Industrial Archaeology and History*, Shire, Aylesbury, 1975
R. A. Buchanan, *Industrial Archaeology in Britain*, Penguin, 1972
Anthony Burton, *Remains of a Revolution*, Deutsch, 1975
H. J. Dyos and D. H. Aldcroft, *British Transport*, Penguin, 1974
W. G. Hoskins, *The Making of the English Landscape*, Penguin, 1970
K. Hudson, *Exploring our Industrial Past*, Hodder, 1975
Roy Palmer, *A Touch on the Times: Songs of Social Change, 1770-1914*, Penguin, 1974
Eric Partridge, *A Dictionary of Historical Slang*, Penguin, 1972
Christopher Pulling, *They Were Singing and What They Sang About*, Harrap, 1952
L. T. C. Rolt, *Isambard Kingdom Brunel*, Penguin, 1970
Victorian Engineering, Penguin, 1974
C. E. R. Sherrington, *100 Years of Inland Transport*, 1934 (reprinted, Cass, 1969)
Jack Simmons, *Journeys in England*, Odhams, 1951

Roads
W. Albert, *The Turnpike Road System in England*, Cambridge University Press, 1972
R. C. and J. M. Anderson, *Quicksilver: A Hundred Years of Coaching, 1750-1850*, David and Charles, 1973
E. W. Bovill, *English Country Life, 1780-1830*, 1962
John Copeland, *Roads and their Traffic*, David and Charles, 1968
A. Everitt, 'Country Carriers in the Nineteenth Century' in *Journal of Transport History*, new series, vol. III, no. 3, February 1976, pp. 179-201
Sir Herbert George Fordham, *The Road-Books and Itineraries of Great Britain, 1750-1850: A Catalogue*, Cambridge University Press, 1924
Neil Grant, *Stagecoaches*, Kestrel, 1977
C. G. Harper, *Stage-Coach and Mail in Days of Yore*, 2 vols, Chapman and Hall, 1903
Stella Margetson, *Journey by Stages*, Cassell, 1967
Morris Marples, *Shanks's Pony*, Country Book Club, 1960
David Mountfield, *The Coaching Age*, Hale, 1976
Eric Pawson, *Transport and Economy: the Turnpike Roads of Eighteenth Century Britain*, Academic Press, 1977
John Richards, *Stagecoach: the Real Story of Coaching*, Watmoughs Ltd, 1976
Peter Smith, *The Turnpike Age*, Luton Museum and Art Gallery, 1971
W. Outram Tristram, *Coaching Days and Coaching Ways*, 1894

Canals
Anthony Burton, *The Canal Builders*, Methuen, 1972
The Navigators (novel), Macdonald and Jane's, 1976
R. M. Evans, *Communications in South Wales: Canals, 1800-1920* (folder of documents), National Museum of Wales, Cardiff, 1975
Charles Hadfield, *The Canal Age*, Pan, 1971
H. Hanson, *The Canal Boatmen, 1760-1914*, Manchester University Press, 1975
J. D. Porteous, *Canal Ports*, Academic Press, 1977
Jon Raven, *Canal Songs*, Broadside Records, 1974
L. T. C. Rolt, *Narrow Boat*, Methuen, 1944
George Smith, *Our Canal Population*, 1875 (new edition of 1878, reprinted, E. P. Publishing, Wakefield, 1975)
Peter Smith, *Waterways Heritage*, Luton Museum and Art Gallery, 1972

Railways
J. W. Carmichael, *Views on the Newcastle and Carlisle Railway 1836-8* (reprinted, Frank Graham, Newcastle, 1969)
Terry Coleman, *The Railway Navvies*, Penguin, 1968
S. C. Dean and R. M. Gard, *The Stockton and Darlington Railway, 1825* (folder of documents), University of Newcastle upon Tyne, Department of Education, 1975
Alan Delgado, *The Annual Outing*, Allen and Unwin, 1976
R. M. Evans, *Communications in South Wales: Railways, 1800-1920* (folder of documents), National Museum of Wales, Cardiff, 1975

R. M. Gard and J. R. Hartley, *Railways in the Making* (folder of documents), University of Newcastle upon Tyne, Department of Education, 1969
W. R. Mitchell and N. J. Mussett, *Seven Years Hard: Building the Settle – Carlisle Railway*, Dalesman, Clapham, 1976
Patrick MacGill, *Children of the Dead End: The Autobiography of a Navvy*, 1914
G. Ottley, *Bibliography of British Railway History*, Allen and Unwin, 1965
Harold Perkin, *The Age of the Railway*, Panther, 1970
Report of the Select Committee on Railway Labourers, Parliamentary Papers, vol. XIII, 1846
L. T. C. Rolt, *Red for Danger*, 1955
Jack Simmons, *The Railways of Britain*, Routledge, 1955
David Stevenson, *Fifty Years on the L.N.W.R.*, 1891
F. S. Williams, *Our Iron Roads*, 1852

The Sea
E. H. H. Archibald, *Travellers by Sea*, H.M.S.O., 1962
Richard Armstrong, *Powered Ships*, Benn, 1975
B. D. Beckett, *Shanties and Forebitters*, 1914
R. C. Bell, *Diaries from the Days of Sail*, Barrie and Jenkins, 1974
F. T. Bullen, *The Men of the Merchant Service*, 1900
F. T. Bullen and W. F. Arnold, *Songs of Sea Labour*, 1914
Susan Campbell-Jones, *Welsh Sail*, Gomer Press Ltd, Llandysul, Dyfed, Wales, 1976
Sir Francis Chichester, *Along the Clipper Way*, Pan, 1967
Joanna C. Colcord, *Roll and Go: Songs of American Sailormen*, Bobbs-Merrill, Indianapolis, 1924
Terry Coleman, *Passage to America*, Penguin, 1972
Captain Fred W. Ellis, *Round Cape Horn in Sail*, Croydon, 1949
John Fowles, *Shipwreck*, Cape, 1974
Alison Grant, *Sailing Ships and Emigrants in Victorian Times*, Longman, 1972
Basil Greenhill, *The Great Migration*, National Maritime Museum, 1976
Thomas M. Hemy, *Deep Sea Days*, 1926
Captain J. W. Holmes, *Voyaging*, Hutchinson, 1965
F. E. Huggett, *Life and Work at Sea*, Harrap, 1975
Stan Hugill, *Shanties from the Seven Seas*, Routledge, 1965
M. A. Jones, *Destination America*, Weidenfeld, 1976
Peter Kemp (ed.) *The Oxford Companion to Ships and the Sea*, Oxford University Press, 1976
Frank Knight, *The Clipper Ship*, Collins, 1973
A. B. Lubbock, *Round the Horn*, 1903
The Western Ocean Packets, 1925
Philip McCutchan, *Tall Ships*, Weidenfeld, 1976
John Masefield, *Bird of Dawning* (novel), 1933
Eric Newby, *The Last Grain Race*, Pan, 1972
John O'Callaghan, *The Saga of the SS. 'Great Britain'*, Hart-Davis, 1971
Captain Walter H. Parker, *Leaves from an Unwritten Logbook*, 1931
George Peters, *The Plimsoll Line: A Biography of Samuel Plimsoll*, Barry Rose, 1975
Charles Protheroe, *Life in the Mercantile Marine*, 1903
Captain Samuel Samuels, *From Forecastle to Cabin*, New York, 1887
M. R. Savage and A. G. Thompson, *The Tyne, 1800-1850* (folder of documents), University of Newcastle upon Tyne, Department of Education, 1970
Andrew Shewan, *The Great Days of Sail*, 1927 (reprinted, Conway Maritime Press, 1973)
James Sibree, *Fifty Years' Recollections*, Hull, 1884

L. A. Smith, *Music of the Waters*, 1888
Michael Stammers, *Liverpool Shipping* (folder of documents), Scouse Press, 4 Windermere Terrace, Liverpool 8, n.d.
F. W. H. Symondson, *Two Years Abaft the Mast, or, Life as a Sea Apprentice*, Edinburgh, 1876
W. R. Thrower, *Life at Sea in the Age of Sail*, Phillimore, 1972
Alan Villiers, *The Cruise of the 'Conrad'*, Pan, 1973
Captain W. B. Whall, *Sea Songs and Shanties*, Brown, Son and Ferguson, Glasgow, 1963

School projects

An immense amount of research remains to be done. The history of local turnpike trusts, canals, railway lines or branch lines, emigration from small ports; all these can be illuminated from archives, newspaper files, and in some cases from oral recollections and traditions. Work of this kind can also shed a good deal of light on particular incidents and events. For example, the railway accident near Abergele, the subject of the song *Railway Passengers burnt to death*, on page 48, does not figure in Rolt's work, *Red for Danger*. Local and, indeed, national newspapers must have reported it. It may be that there are people in the area who have handed down family stories about it. Perhaps some local autobiographer mentioned it. There could be photographs in a local museum. The site of the accident may still exist. Material obtained in this way can be presented in a booklet, a folder of documents in facsimile, an exhibition, a documentary with music, or in a combination of all these. The technique can be widely applied.

Sources

Songs and tunes

1. Text: broadside printed 'for J. G. by J. Marshall, Newcastle' (Newcastle upon Tyne University Broadside Collection, Box 2, Folder 9). I am grateful to Jon Raven for communicating this text. Tune not indicated; I have used *The Swaggering Lads o' Percy Main* (G. and M. Polwarth, *Folk Songs from the North*, Frank Graham, Newcastle, 1970, p. 54).
2. Text: G. Greig, *Folk-Song of the North-East*, 2 vols, Peterhead, 1909 and 1914; no. VII. Tune: collected by Greig from A. Robb (Greig MSS in Aberdeen University Library). I am grateful to Pat Shaw for communicating this and other versions.
3. Text: C. G. Harper, *Stage-Coach and Mail in Days of Yore*, 2 vols, Chapman and Hall, 1903; vol. I, pp. 317-18. I am grateful to Mr John Richards for this reference. Tune: *Here's to the Maiden* (W. Chappell, *Popular Music of the Olden Time*, 1859, p. 744).
4. Text: broadside printed by W. Collard, Bridewell Lane, and Hotwells, Bristol (BL LR 271 a 2, vols. I-II, p. 89). Collard was printing at this address between 1818 and 1835. I have adapted and abridged the text. Tune not indicated; I have used a version of *The Golden Glove* (Frank Kidson, *Traditional Tunes*, 1891, p. 173).
5. Text: broadside printed by W. Pratt of Birmingham (Kidson Broadside Collection, Mitchell Library, Glasgow, vol. II, p. 75). It bears the stock number 427. Pratt was printing from about 1850 to 1862. Tune: sung by Fred Jordan of Aston Munslow, Salop; collected in Birmingham by Roy Palmer, 1966.

6. Text: *Stamford Mercury*, 17 May 1793. I am grateful to Mr Michael Honeybone for communicating this text. Tune not indicated; I have used a popular tune of the day, *Nancy Dawson* (Chappell, *op. cit.*, p. 719).
7. Broadside without imprint (Newcastle upon Tyne University Broadside Collection, Box 3). I am grateful to Jon Raven for drawing this to my attention by printing it in facsimile in his *Canal Songs*, Broadside Records, 1974, p.13. Tune not indicated; I have used the tune of an analogous song, *Paddy's Balloon* (Davidson's *Universal Melodist*, n.d., vol. I, p. 259).
8. Text: Liverpool Record Office; abridged. Tune: from memory; source untraced.
9. Text: broadside printed by W. Boag of Newcastle, over the initials, J. G., South Shields (private collection). I am grateful to Edward Thompson for communicating this text. Tune: *Patrick O'Neal* (based on the version in the Sam Henry Collection, no. 554, Belfast Public Library).
10. Text: broadside printed by Willey of Cheltenham (Madden Collection, Cambridge University Library); abridged. Tune not indicated; I have used *Jolly Fellows that Follow the Plough* (S. Baring-Gould, *Songs of the West*, Methuen, 1905, p. 130).
11. Text: John Stoyls, originally published in the *Stockport Magazine*, 1840. Reprinted by Samuel Hill in *Old Lancashire Songs and their Singers*, Manchester, 1906, pp. 21-23. Tune: Roy Palmer.
12. Text: broadside printed by Harkness of Preston, set by Roy Palmer to the tune of *The Piper's Tunes* (*Touch on the Times*, Penguin, 1974, p. 40).
13. Text: Greig, *op. cit.*, no. XII, p. 2. Tune: Sung by J. W. Spence; collected by Gavin Greig, April, 1904 (MS in Aberdeen University Library). I am grateful to Pat Shaw for communicating this tune.
14. Text: broadside printed by H. Such, 177 Union Street, London (Harding Collection, Bodleian Library). Tune (a) for the verse: under the title of *Paddy from Home* in A. B. Gomme, *The Traditional Games of England, Scotland, and Ireland*, 2 vols, 1894-98; vol. II, p. 36; (b) for the chorus: sung, with a fragmentary text, entitled *The Greenock Railway*, by A. Robb; collected by Gavin Greig (MS in Aberdeen University Library). I am grateful to Pat Shaw for communicating this tune. I have married these four-line tunes from different versions, since to repeat either one for the twelve lines of verse and chorus would have been monotonous.
15. Text and tune: broadside published by R. W. Hume, *The Lyre No. 105 Steam-ery* (Harding Collection, Bodleian Library). The music has been adapted.
16. Text: broadside printed by W. Taylor, 39 Temple Street, Bristol (Madden Collection, 23/382, Cambridge University Library). Tune not indicated; I have used a version of *The Jolly Roving Tar* which apparently dates back to the early 1840s (Sam Henry Collection, no. 670).
17. Sung by Mr James Sutton at Winterton, Norfolk; collected by E. J. Moeran, July 1915 (*Journal of the English Folk Song Society*, vol. VII, p. 6). The text has been filled out from a broadside without imprint, *Wreck of the Royal Charter* (Street Ballad Collection, Brown, Picton and Hornsby Libraries, Liverpool).
18. Text: broadside printed by T. Pearson, 4 and 6 Chadderton Street, Manchester (Ballad Collection Q 398.8 S.9, vol. II, p. 615, Manchester Central Library). Tune: *Driven from Home* (communicated by the Westminster City Librarian).
19. From the singing of Roy Harris on the record, *The Bitter and the Sweet* (Topic 12TS217, 1972).

Prose passages

Note. Many of the extracts have been abridged and more lightly punctuated.

Anon., 'Autobiography of a Navvy' in *Macmillan's Magazine*, vol. v, 1861-2 (partly reprinted in John Burnett, *Useful Toil*, Allen Lane, 1974; Penguin, 1977)
Sir Francis Bond Head, *Stokers and Pokers: Or The London and North-Western Railway*, 1849 (4th edn)
Arthur Brazier, *West Twickenham in the 1890s: A Railwayman's Memories*, Borough of Twickenham Local History Society, 1976
R. Chambers, *Book of Days*, 2 vols, 1862-3
E. D. Cuming (ed.), *Squire Osbaldeston: His Autobiography*, Bodley Head, 1926
William Derricourt (or Day), *Old Convict Days*, ed. G. L. Becke, 1899
Charles Dickens, *Dombey and Son*, 1848
The Old Curiosity Shop, 1841
Article in *All the Year Round*, 28 January 1860, reprinted in *The Uncommercial Traveller*, 1875
Charles Greville, *Memoirs*, ed. H. Reeve, 1896
G. Hamilton Ellis, *British Railway History*, Allen and Unwin, vol. I, *1830-1876*, 1954 and vol II, *1877-1947*, 1959.
John Hollinghead, 'On the Canal' in *Household Words*, vol. 18, 1858
William Hone, *Every-day and Table Book*, 3 vols, 1838
William Hutton, *An History of Birmingham to 1780*, first published, 1782, 1795 (3rd edn.)
Peter Lecount, *The History of the Railways Connecting London and Birmingham*, 1839
F. G. Llewellin, *The Lighter Side of a Parson's Life*, Adams and Sons, Hereford, n.d.
John Metcalf, *The Life of John Metcalf*, Leeds, 1801 (2nd edn)
M. C. F. Morris, *Yorkshire Reminiscences*, 1922
W. H. Pyne, *Microcosm*, 1808
H. C. Robinson, *Diary, Reminiscences and Correspondence*, ed. T. Sadler, 1872 (3rd edn)
George Sorrell, *Man Before the Mast*, Methuen, 1928.
Swinney's Chronicle, in *Local Notes and Queries*, Birmingham Reference Library, no. 394945
The Times, 27 October 1809
Ralph Whitlock, *A Family and a Village*, Baker, 1969

Illustrations

Cover, p.17 *Illustrated London News*, photograph Cambridge University Library; pp.5,6,9,29 Mansell Collection; p.1,15 The National Museum of Wales; p.12 The Post Office; p.13 The Guildhall Library, City of London, photograph by Arthur Vialls; p.18 British Rail (Western Region); p.21 The Waterways Museum, Stoke Bruerne; p. 24 Kidson Collection, Mitchell Library, Glasgow; p.25 From F. S. Williams, *The Midland Railway*, 1876, photograph Cambridge University Library; pp.31,41,47 photographs Science Museum, London; p.35 Photograph by the Bromsgrove Messenger Newspaper; p.37 The National Railway Museum; pp.40,57,61 Radio Times Hulton Picture Library; p.43 Sutcliffe Gallery, Whitby; p.45 Central Library, Newcastle upon Tyne; p.48 The British Library; p.49 From T. A. Croal, *A Book about Travelling*, 1877, photograph Cambridge University Library; p.53 National Maritime Museum, London; p.55 Merseyside County Museums; p.56 Photograph R. Rees Lewis.

For EU product safety concerns, contact us at Calle de José Abascal, 56–1°,
28003 Madrid, Spain or eugpsr@cambridge.org.

www.ingramcontent.com/pod-product-compliance
Ingram Content Group UK Ltd.
Pitfield, Milton Keynes, MK11 3LW, UK
UKHW051916230326
469290UK00012B/204